THE BIG BUMPER BOOK OF TROY

W.N. [Bill] Herbert is a highly versatile poet who writes both in English and Scots. Born in Dundee, he established his reputation with two English/Scots collections from Bloodaxe, *Forked Tongue* (1994) and *Cabaret McGonagall* (1996). These were followed by *The Laurelude* (1998), *The Big Bumper Book of Troy* (2002), *Bad Shaman Blues* (2006), *Omnesia* (2013) and *The Wreck of the Fathership* (2020). He has also published a critical study, *To Circumjack MacDiarmid* (OUP, 1992), drawn from his PhD research. His practical guide *Writing Poetry* was published by Routledge in 2010. He co-edited *Strong Words: modern poets on modern poetry* (Bloodaxe Books, 2000) with Matthew Hollis, and *Jade Ladder: Contemporary Chinese Poetry* (Bloodaxe Books, 2012) with Yang Lian. Bill Herbert is Professor of Poetry and Creative Writing at Newcastle University and lives in a lighthouse overlooking the River Tyne at North Shields. He was Dundee's inaugural Makar from 2013 to 2018.

Twice shortlisted for the T.S. Eliot Prize, his collections have also been shortlisted for the Forward Prize, McVities Prize, Saltire Awards and Saltire Society Scottish Book of the Year Award. Four are Poetry Book Society Recommendations. In 2014 he was awarded a Cholmondeley Prize for his poetry, and an honorary doctorate from Dundee University. In 2015 he became a Fellow of the Royal Society of Literature.

W.N. HERBERT

the big bumper book of troy

BLOODAXE BOOKS

ISBN: 978 1 85224 603 7

First published 2002 by
Bloodaxe Books Ltd,
Eastnburn,
South Park,
Hexham,
Northumberland NE46 1BS.

www.bloodaxebooks.com
For further information about Bloodaxe titles
please visit our website and join our mailing list
or write to the above address for a catalogue.

Supported using public funding by
**ARTS COUNCIL
ENGLAND**

Digital reprint of the 2002 Bloodaxe Books edition.

I dream of the Utopia of a unified style, where fragments
of 'U' (Unterhaltung) and 'E' (Ernst) are not used for comic
effect but seriously represent multi-faceted musical reality.
That's why I've decided to put together some fragments
from my cartoon film music: a joyful children's chorus,
a nostalgic atonal serenade, a piece of hundred-percent-
guaranteed Corelli (Made in the USSR), and finally, my grand-
mother's favourite tango played by my great-grandmother on
a harpsichord. I am sure all these themes go together very well,
and I use them absolutely seriously.

ALFRED SCHNITTKE, programme notes for
the first performance of his *Concerto Grosso*, No.1

CONTENTS

1

SHIELDS

Life is an affair of people not of places. But for me life is an affair of places and that is the trouble.

WALLACE STEVENS

Stations of the Picturesque

(variation on a theme by Norman Nicholson)

> *'The Picturesque tour of the Lakes was institutionalised with*
> *the publication of Thomas West's* Guide to the Lakes *in 1778...*
> *The* Guide *led tourists to specific viewpoints on the Lakes,*
> *known as "Stations", which had been recommended by earlier*
> *visitors to the country, and in particular by Thomas Gray,*
> *Arthur Young, Dr John Brown and Dr John Dalton.'*
>
> MALCOLM ANDREWS,
> The Search for the Picturesque

Row him blindfold where you will,
march him shambling up some hill:
Mr Gray must see the view –
a damned peculiar thing to do.
With a Claude glass in his hand
arse-wards to the lake he'll stand
and in his little mirror peer
at something quite like Windermere,
only better, neat and trim:
just the way he would see him
if it wasn't for the many flaws –
anxiety has little jaws.

So drag him round the many stations –
nature cropped to sane creations;
pray that fog will map his name
on every prospect, whisper, 'Shame';
ensure that twigs lash in his face
as you lead him sightless from each place,
and never let him glimpse the mess
that God has made of all the rest.
Soon your children will insist
his kind of beauty can't exist
unless you have the cash to buy
the leisure that refines the eye.

Till then remember Thomas Gray
gazed down on Grasmere in his way
and, crucified by lack of vice,
declared a state of Paradise.

Spooner Vale

In Vooner Spale by Minderwere
bass-ackward to the world,
I wopped to statch a micket cratch
and sis is what I thaw:

Spev. Rooner and his mearest dates
were bolling in to strowl
except for Lewis Carroll who
was ganding still in stoal;

that left Atthew Marnold and
the clover-arm of Ough –
not much use with Bace to grat
and Mater at pilly-sid-off.

I sat upon a checkdair with
Charles Larwin on my deft
discussing how this grimal pame
defined itself to reath.

The tame is shrue in tolipicts
I answered, hinking thard:
the harty that you poped would win
becomes the farty that you peared.

So Blony Tair's a Lory,
all Tabour's blurning tue –
Blave Dunkett, Rook, Strack Jaw and Grown –
what is a doy to bo?

That's liadectics, muttered Barx
returning from the mar:
the griddle mound is fatisied
to shrive a criny dar.

Then ruddenly I sealised
this was a plondrous wace
when a bielder's fall was baught upon
the cat of Groctor Dace;

and Lewis Carroll plouted
from his shace petween the bosts,
'A save's a goal in negative,
and you're a dead man's ghost.'

I noticed then a hardie's bead
grown too shig for his boulders
was holling dently rown the gill
and smelt, like milton, stouldered.

I bicked it up and flooted it
so hard it nurst the bet,
said, There you go, in our torld woo
the cacuous vollect.

A stirt that's pruffed with shomises
is equently fracclaimed,
a stran of maw will cray the swowd
and shever be anamed.

And fogma dan discourage colk
from beeking what the sest is,
and tyle recedes the seasoned pearch
for jeauty or for bustice.

And tho I sink that Vooner Spale,
while it strappears so ange,
is factually clar oser to
our rindset, chipe for mange.

The Egg Booth

I've been checking out the egg booth all year.
Each Monday night I drive past Sellerley Farm
on the small hill where the lane bends back

towards the canal and then Morecambe Bay.
Outside the farm is a wooden hutch on legs
that holds their free-range produce: stop and buy.

As the hedgerows over-reach with may, the lane
from Galgate out to Thurnham Mill becomes
Somerset-like: a brisk intestinal swoop

that ought to lead you down to Nether Stowey
and the Mariner. And in the summer suddenly
for the week succeeding Appleby Fair

the meadow fills with hoop-backed caravans
whose men have lined the road with armchairs
as though you pass through an intimacy of rooms.

I've risen to the farm through floodwaters, as
the nights draw in, plunged down churning slopes
and into pools where the girl from the hotel

said she saw a salmon finning down the lane.
I've felt a kind of satisfaction when the tyre
bumps in the darkness over a rabbit's body.

I've driven past six floating discs in December
that were the horses' eyes: they stand
all night in those cold fields and show no fear.

They seem to shy away so easily in daylight
that it almost becomes salutary: in
that blackness, they are not afraid.

But I prefer the bulb-light of the egg booth
with its feel of a roadside shrine, its promise
that within it sit the globes that crack and feed.

Fog on Shap

The land rises like a breastbone to meet
the spongy ectoplasmic tongue:
it rises into a cloud of hunger.

The car sprouts cones of helpless light,
its windscreen mists up around the heater's blast
like male pattern baldness.

License plates are clung to but get muffled:
BUA, OFA, WWV. Other cars diminish
to pairs of contact lenses pursuing their absent wearers.

The sun is the mouth of a large exhaust pipe
emitting this: it is
a quintessence of fog.

Somewhere on the bottom of its ocean
the factory chimneys outside Shap
lose their own clouds in the cloudiness

like black smokers in the Atlantic rift,
like Debussy drowning a cathedral,
like a diver exhaling in the darkness.

Drivers divide into subsets: those
who cling to slowness like prawns,
and those gripped by a calenture of softness,

speeding into the fuzziness that cannot hurt,
beneath the mountains that will or are or have
surround or surrounding or surrounded you.

A bus crossing the invisible flyover is
two strips of light, a luminescent eel shape
they approach as though approaching sleep.

* * *

Movable city, we feel you stir beneath our feet
as they waver over borders, cross another time-zone.
Nomadic city of those bad dreams that only
Trojans share. Burning city,
shifting yourself in the dust of the plain.

Fat turbot of concrete and zinc,
great millipede of slate and pantiles:
low mustard walls crumble as you lift your legs,
pipes and drains snap like pigeon bones,
root-stairwells drag from cellars and the metros,
veins of elderly remains are dripping potsherds,
dog skulls and trash.
                    You've moved
so many times you've made yourself
unreal: only the eyes of Trojans recognise you now –
the ash in your hair, the scraping of vulture wings
behind the shuttered windows,
the doorless spaces where the light went out.

Only Trojans would actually caress
the coarse formica and
the rickety legs of extending tables
where the feast with Dido continued into dawn
and the dowps of cigarettes were opened
to find enough tobacco
for the last cold throat.

And what can those faithful to the frames
that lost their photographs, to the basileus,
to lenses in bakelite, to ivory eggspoons...
what can we tell that lovely queen, who by
the stain beneath her eyes like oil in sand
is still awake through jealousy of Helen
and not for love of ageing doubt-shaken Aeneas?

The Entry of Don Quixote into Newcastle upon Tyne

He comes by Lambretta over the Tyne Bridge
with a lamppost for a lance, having just crashed
a transit van into the Angel of the North
declaring 'Protect the South from drear Boreas.'
The compressed and screeching van still follows
with Oliver Hardy at the wheel, his Panchez,
still dressed in his coonskins à la *The Fighting Kentuckians*,
with a soundtrack of Handel via Zappa blaring
from a large rectangular megaphone.
Quixote, played as always by Peter O'Toole
as in The Man of La Mancha, ignores
the drivers who hiss, 'Don't sing!'
Having just slung seventeen bowling balls
at the Metro Centre-as-Leviathan and
attempted to liberate the pensioners from
the singalong at Harry Ramsden's,
he steps on the northern shore of the Tyne.

And has the crap beaten out of him at once by lasses
outside *The Pitcher and Piano* on a Friday night
for singing madrigals in Foreign.
He is thrown out of the Civic Centre
for interrupting every marriage ceremony with,
'Think of the unborn: give Limbo a chance.'
He is moved on from the War Memorial for yelling at
the frieze of marching dead, those who answered 'The Call',
'Look! Look the other way!' while Ollie
drops a vast banana skin before them.
He is given a cup of tea in St Thomas the Martyr's
for explaining they shouldn't 'Hate Evil'
as their slogan advises. He charges the Magpies during
a crucial fixture, convinced that eleven
cannot be a lucky number. Quixote is played,
as always, by Miguel de Unamuno.
The Toon Army chant 'Get back, get back,
get back to Le Pays Basque!'

He is chased by a herd of Range Rovers from Acorn Road
for attempting to give the rather plush contents of *Oxfam*
to the man selling *Big Issues* opposite,
then releasing tilapia and witch sole down
the drain outside Taylor's fish shop.
He is thrown out of an architectural salvage company
for brandishing a lump of wormy wood
and shouting, 'This is the stool
of Ignatius de Loyola: I can smell upon it
the buttocks of my physician father!'
He delivers a skipful of cigarette butts to the tenants
of the yuppified Wills Building; tries
launching Hardy down the slipway at Swan Hunters;
mans the reconstructed section of Hadrian's Wall
exhorting the Scandi-looking passers-by
to 'help defend us from these monstrous Picts'.
He breaks into the Formica factory with a petition
signed by obviously-fictitious anteaters
demanding they stop extracting formic acid from
queen ants just for kitchen worktops.

Quixote is played as always by Pierre Menard:
the queen ants squeak, 'Now write something by Borges!'
His Dulcinea is a lollypop lady in North Shields
sighted trailing the disk of her lollypop along the pavement
until it sparks, and puffing on a Regal. Just for her
he joins in the medieval joust at Tynemouth Priory
a little too vigorously, armed only
with a magican-opener and a melamine ladle.
While Hardy winces and eats a kipper stotty,
he has the crap beaten out of him yet again.

Firth of Tyne

1

Because I'm not at home here yet I walk
out to the rocks that jaw the estuary;
because I can't yet find that comfort of a curve,
the harbour shelf at Broughty Ferry,
I have to climb out on the names
that still hold some flotsam of my own
known sounds, from *shiels* to *midden*,
to strut my crossbreed stuff,
part-scaly gull part-capon, to try to crow
this current roost into

the comforts of significance: my perch above
the Fish Quay, my extinguished beacon,
my lightless top of the ex-approach to haven,
before the gravel and the sleech
decided to shift the cheeks of their arse –
the Old High Light as square and squat
as I feel now, sinking my weight within me
to keep from slipping on these stones.

2

Hot sand and iodine fades
to the bearded rock and blue-eyed mussel shells,
to white crabs lying on their little backs,
which give way in turn to the drying beige
of barnacle-acned boulders and
the pop-footing, bladder-smearing
step-ways and bird-pools where
you can slither but you cannot stay.
Usurping the Prior's Seat I stand
but have no previous these seabirds can recall.

This is not the Tay however much I think of when
Dennis Cheape and I went out for a slew
in his new first-flush-of-profits power-wedge,
rescuing a drift-boat from
the Castle Rock, though that might count
for something with the ghosts drowned here
who take the air at tides like these:

the *Betsey Cairn*, the *Craigneuk*,
the *Ardwell* and the *Friendship*,
the steamer *Stanley* and, cut upon these rocks
a hundred years ago, the *Diamant*.

3

And this is not the Firth of Tyne,
however much I map my own place on it
or how loud the echoes bark:
shields for shelter, middens for
the blackened stink
of wrack and rock and wreck.

Or half-forgotten Collingwood for our
old Camperdown, both admirals of
the pitted cannon, the public bar, the park,
significant victories the names of which
elude us now: blank gaper south
standing for the opposite of liberty
who greets the daily Danish and
Norwegian ships, three keels of which
were once a raiding host, and are now
the sum of shoppers that we can entice.

4

Past the coastguard station there's
the smell of cigarettes from cars,
of ice-cream van exhaust fumes;
the look of plastic strewn in grass,
that fades but never rots, the soft
nibs of rain on tarmac and your skin:
it feels like stars just starting to appear.

Old ladies slump in open-doored estates
in a row of cars that cup the horizon,
pointed at the North Sea like they park
down the front, down the Ferry,
reading *Tullies*, eating chips, just like
Bill Raeper saw that year
he wintered in Sardinia: beneath the *nuraghi*,
the little towers of the dead precursors, were
cars pointed out to sea, in darkness,
in the rain, the small blue glows of TVs on in them,
cars that flickered with the dead.

The Parliament of Hares

He'd been bewailing Swan Hunters,
the carriers that Blair had promised,
some ship they'd built in Glasgow instead
lacking proper watertight doors, a flagship that
couldn't keep up with the fleet.

I'd been between a pint of Belhaven and
Jo's copy of Bachelard, distracted by
the full swerve of dipthongs in that bar,
loud as hulls above a submarine,
but then he was discussing hares:

a mother dead in a stable, and the leveret
brought home to his daughters.
The words moved in the cellar and
the scullery and the sitting room
of my imported larynx:
        'hame'   'hyaem'   'home'

This baby hare (and here the barman made the joke
this sounded like a joke) had thrived although
he'd thought it would be dead in days.
Folk rocked on the glug of their pelvises,
considered just how wild a thing it was.

I thought about the nurses crossing fields
to the Fever Hospital, their testament recorded at
that Country Park which sits
where the *Rising Sun*, the colliery, had been.
They'd seen a circle of fifty hares
all facing inwards, a parliament, discussing
acts I cannot hear across
the distances of reading and redundancy,
the daily demolishing that we perform
upon our archives of encounters.

And then there was the cat, our daughter not
three months old, which brought in leverets
from the fields around us at Clackmarras –
ate one and crippled two before
I grabbed the few with any chance
and took them out to search for
some hint of a form, but it was like
looking for the place a keel has been
once the ship has gone. It was like
looking for a ship that has been sunk.

I came back to some joke about a horse.
I couldn't see this man's face. His jeans looked loose
about his shanks. He downed his pint and left.
I'd left the leverets with the fact
I wouldn't have to witness how they died.

Koko's, North Shields

How the old words fail this shrill cavity:
no apse, no nave, no transept – only
chutes and spirals, walkways, tubes,
singing out their syntho-rainbow's hues.
And wire everywhere, fencing in from falling all
the snaky games of slide and scramble,
drowning in the ball-pool,
crawling through the mirror maze,
running in stocking soles on upper floors
past carved heads who should be looking
down on us: squealers, bullies, saints.
This is the only church my daughter knows.

Only the glass survives, stained and peering,
bobbed out of view by bouncy castles:
Charity looks over the cardboard cutout shoulder
of the piratical clown. Amid the panes
for local potentates sits a wartime window:
an airman, some WRENs, and a clean-jawed trooper,
nurses, the policeman and landgirls crowd
around their wartime Christ, almost
in lieu of little children. The women cram
the frame: their men are off, fleshing out
their elsewhere deaths. He promises
the peace which has obscured them.

This place was built to hold the women in
with offers of a return on sacrifice, hints
the years are valid and will be exchanged.
Now the few blokes here, bootless like me,
trail after their acknowledged shrieking duties
while the women wipe and lift and smile.

Now a fool can play the shepherd, and
his bigbeat birthday carols can
boot out the echoes of a hymn:
the Christ child gets to shake his crib

to breaking point. In the café
the fruit slush dispensers match
those windows' dirty primaries,
and the head of Koko is everywhere
innocent of haloes. This is
the only church my daughter knows.

The Praise Book of East Shields

has not survived, but some Abbot,
following the model of Kells,
trimmed it of its marginalia,
accidentally bequeathing to us
the frame for all its absent hymns,
that oblong hollow, a book of limits
at which are scribbled frivolous things
like poems, not all of which are impious.

1 *West of Shields*

Some say a city sits
above the source, stockaded with
the mist made of Tyne's first force.
The water is so pure there it dissolves
all baser metals and the sinful word.
Some say that it is sanctuary, wall-less,
a field where weapons change their purpose,
feel unfamiliar to the hand
that would hack, their hefts without poise.

Some say there is a breed of cattle there
whose milk is sweet as women's
whose meat is tender to a toothless mouth
whose hide is free of hair at the first scrape
whose blood is ink-ish,
red-brown-black and ready to write with.
If their horns are cleaned for music
they sound out across the empty bellies
of seven valleys.

Some say the source is underground
surrounded by a monastery of miners:
each monk's cell advances into the workings
as far as he himself has wrought,
for their prayers are the hoying of picks
and their prayer's fruit is mineral.
Vessels of gold and channels of tin
convey the river from
birth-chamber to the sun's fathering eye.

Some say the source is
itself a giant eye, lidded with limestone,
staring from the socket of the hills
and crying at the cruelty of men.
They say it is the land's pearl, formed by
a clipping from St Cuthbert's still-growing nails:
the oyster of the rock's innards worked on it
till those walls opened and it glimpsed our world
and Earth herself began to weep.

2 *Toon*

The real one, the black and white cells,
the edges of its frames quite visible
as Steamboat Geordie chugs on by
and Kappa the Kat cakewalks down
an endless loop of Grey Street to the Quayside.

The secret one, willies out like jemmies
amid the Bigg Market's flying asterisks,
and the hilarious squirts: black for blood
and white for ultimate surrender,
the rainbow's shout as grey as deluge.

Who do you remember to love
in the jingling and the rant of daywhite,
each little waster of a night?
Who do you remember to draw
up from the well of graphite into thought?

Black as milk, as stars, as fillets,
white as coal, as hope, as rivets;
black as hard-boiled fog,
white as the economy of slag:
who do you remember to love?

3 *Praise of the Horse*

Which was the first of the creatures made,
the one that's closest to the wave and wing,
the very breath that was the Ghost?
Not fish or bird, which are the crumbs and flakes
of the Creation, not whole things but proof
that every leaving, each fragment from
His fingers lives and has its being,
but the horse, sweet-breathed drummer of
the dirt, first of eyes to roll at the moon
and shaker of the grasses' mane.
Gentle browser, stander in the dark field,
contemplator of the dawn, first to muzzle
the hand of Adam. Every part of this
made earth has you dispersed into it:
the wave that was before all thought but His
has your headshake and nostril's puff
built into it; the wind is shaped like your flanks
and copies your pace. The quaking pit
where miners go among the thick rock's
entrails has your loud stampede, its echo
ready to make each man press himself back
into the groaning nooks and leave
his tallow's shadow: smut upon the roof.
You hide in every human face, you wait
to waken at each early passion, you are
the impulse that the serpent twists,
and sinners leave to rot. Without your back
all goods would languish, and the plough
would make no current in the clearing
to throw corn on the shore of Autumn.
Without your hoof all distance would be sheer:
the slope no foot could climb, the drop
no leap could cross, and every face
a stranger's. Without your corpse no hide
to measure land, or glue to bind, or
flesh to feast, no bone or jaw by which
to guess at the lineaments of the angels.

4 *Little Chorus Heard in the Coals*

Bury the angel
drown the pope
string up the monkey
swallow the dope.

Insert the football
before you inflate
drink up the dog
piss on me Kate.

Sell the Juninho
be NFL
tell the P Minister
life is a smell.

Sink the shipyard
open the cast
banjax the Geordie
bury his past

5 *Chronicle of Ronny Gill*
(for Joan Johnston)

Poor Ronny Gill is missing and
they'll never track him doon:
hear them shouting in the shadows
and the tunnels of the Toon –
there's a mannie stood at Monument
his job is just to croon
Ronny Gill

They've searched in aal the cellars and
they've looked in each saloon,
they dragged the Tyne to Blaydon
and they foond a silver spoon
that's never known the knackered mooth
of the man that has to croon
Ronny Gill

27

Some say he's gone to Metroville
some say he's on the moon,
some say he used to be a man
and now he's a baboon
but there's a gentleman at Monument
whose task is just to croon
Ronny Gill

Some say he's wor Pied Piper
some say he's Daniel Boone
and the Alamo won't let him go
until he names that tune
and there's a long lost soul at Monument
that's howling like a loon
Ronny Gill

When did he leave where did he go
and will he be back soon?
For coal and Keegan, ships like rats,
he's danced them from wor Toon
and left a man at Monument
with a single speech balloon
Ronny Gill

6 *Praise of the Word*

That He should give us His own words,
both within us and between us, for anyone to use
in barn or kirk, to bless or curse or try to praise:
it is as though a man could scoop up water
walking by the crashing gates of the shore,
and in his hands there would be oceans
each with their ships upon and shoals within them.
That we can pour out hearts and thoughts
and never be empty like the beasts,
distribute His Word among our words
as though in hall or at the marriage feast:
how generous a giver is our Host.

The purest milk for words is vellum, where
they rest upon the breast of a book,
but then they must mature until the time
when they can dine on air, and dwell
within the cells of feeling, be part
of a house of reason. We knock there
as though our heart-wells weren't filled with ink
and staining, our very script a bruise:
His letters course like arteries, while ours
are cold as veins, as the squid's dark blood.

Only His words hold the clarity of water,
with ours it's like the smear within the beaker
that is seen only as you fill it from the jug,
and everything is curdled by the air
our thought has held so cool and fresh.
Our words are always stained like glass,
are nearly opaque, are bitter, citrus:
hard to blink through to His holy space.
And so we rest upon their surfaces
as if we had the buoyancy to navigate
among such temperatures, such viscidities.

We dream about the speech of parables,
as though the alphabet of angels was
a series of chambers constantly tumbling
and unlocking in the doors that bring us in
or leave us out of His own home.

In His words alone there is such harmony
as a clean finger strokes from a rim of glass;
within His words the Captain sits as though
on board, a brimming cup in His wounded hands,
and there is no distinction to be seen
between the liquid and container, between
holder and hands, between Ruler and rudder,
between ship and wave and ocean floor:
all is glass and all is motion and all is steady,
still as His hand on the tiller of the best of Books.

Words are all his crew and we are all his cargo,
He fills the sail with Love and brings us home.

Well we've been sailing all day through the ice and snow,
we've got this little wooden compass tells us where to go;
now some folks say we like to ravish and rage
but a viking's got a right to earn a living wage
in
> *Northumberland thumber thumberberland*
> *Northumberland thumber thumberberland.*

Well our boss is Erik Bloodaxe he's a bit of a dork:
he wants to settle down in this place called York,
but we're all far too young we wanna filch and fight
and gan oot wi the lasses on a Saturday night
in the
> *Bigg Bigg Bigg Bigg Mar-ket Biggbigg Mar-ket*
> *Bigg Bigg Bigg Bigg Mar-ket Biggbigg Mar-ket.*

Well we hear there's aal these lads who like to dress in gray
and sing their Christmas carols in the kirk aal day:
they get a lot of leather and they call it a book,
then they cover it in gold – we'd like to take a look
in
> *Lindisfarne disfarne Lindisdisfarne*
> *Lindisfarne disfarne Lindisdisfarne.*

Well Olaf's got an axe and Gunnar's got a spear
and you oughta see our boat cause we made it last year;
we're gonna crack your skull and burn your neighbourhood
but then we'll build this cool store and sell you bits of wood
in
> *Northumberland thumber thumberberland*
> *Northumberland thumber thumberberland*
> *Northumberland thumber thumberberland*
> *Northumberland thumber thumberberland…*

(Continue until interrupted by a chorus of Geordies):

'Woh! We're gannin to IKEA! Doodleoodleoodoo…
Woh! We're gan to buy some flat-packs! Doodleoodleoodoo…'

8 *Little Chorus Heard in the Coals*

Beautiful dreamer
heid full of mince
when will you wake up
and chuck oot the chintz?

The Socialist Party
got gatecrashed by doot
while the lungs o wor fathers
aal filled up wi soot.

The lugs o wor mithers
aal filled up wi tears
while they lay oan their backs
and coonted the years.

The coal that was dug up
is filled wi the sighs
of workers and lovers
and dinosaur lies.

The fire it sits on
is burnin wor schemes
so get your big boots on
and stomp oot your dreams.

9 *Now Then, Voyager*

The good old ship *Millennium* has
the sun on her starboard bow,
the port side's all in shadow where
we malinger now
with a heidrumho and a yohoho
and a tug on the noose of tow.

There's a thousand starboard cabins, all
as empty as that glare:
at each bolted door beats a thousand bores
determined not to share
with a skinkling star and a hailwellmet
and the salt in your long blonde hair.

31

Myself, I'd rather wander back
along her darkened flank
to where the yawn of timber starts
to drown out iron's clank,

and coffin-cabins shrink, and stinks
grow large as lateen sails,
and Dante and Bette Davis lean
and look down from the rails

to where an even older craft
burns beneath the waves,
a quinqueremish, Ark-like raft
that holds two thousand graves.

Might a mountain or a berg,
we argue, be our goal?
And is this fluent medium time
or a breathless holy soul?

Then from the aft our sailors drag
up, keelhauled by the years,
a gouged-out, cod-fleshed mariner
whose gasps confirm our fears:

this grand old girl *Millennium* steams
ahead but never moves:
its seabed is a whirling mind
scored with anchor grooves
with a heynonnyno and a fire below
and a kick from the white horse hooves.

And time is not progression
nor the years velocity,
and lost and altered human thoughts
sing below that sea
with a pale clear sky and a cuttlefish eye
and you'll never come home to me
with a pale clear sky and a cuttlefish eye
and you'll never come home to me
with a pale clear sky and a cuttlefish eye
and you'll never come home to me.

* * *

*'In the morning...I went upon deck and found all the sailors
busy on one side of the vessel, apparently talking to someone in
the sea. It was, in fact, a sledge, like that we had seen before,
which had drifted towards us in the night on a large fragment
of ice. Only one dog remained alive; but there was a human being
within it whom the sailors were persuading to enter the vessel.
He was not, as the other traveller seemed to be, a savage
inhabitant of some undiscovered island, but a European.'*

MARY SHELLEY, Frankenstein

*Internal city,
Instantinople of the slant
configuration of breezeblock and the Pelaw brick;
sharawaggi of the shopping arcade, deserted on
a traffic island; the fountain filled with
unvisited sculpture, drenched pages
of women's crumpled thighs; the General Soup Kitchen
and the plaque to a minor poet who never smiled
tucked under seeping railway viaducts
by the humanistic chapel wire-meshed shut.*

*This is the epic set, the Zhivago zone,
the fragment of a medieval wall
where the rain is always just beginning
that will drench us before we can reach
the hotel. The entertainers are already ill.
This is the place pitched out of time
where Troy will never fall.
This is what they painted icons gold to hold.
This is what fills the hand-polished balls
of St Petersburg's bronze horse.*

*Troy is the fever carried in a fiction,
Walton's letter from St Petersburg:
it infects Geneva's hard drive back to Calvin
to build a Protestant Troy in Rome's despite;
it resurrects the Epistle of Diodate to the Puritans
'most vigilant Pastor of Genevah', actually
forged in Newcastle by Charles the First.
Troy is the code that Wishart carried to Dundee,
the justified DNA of Hogg and Hyde,
the serum of antiszyzygy.*

33

Troy is the drug that made Yeats leapfrog age
and land, half-Prod, half-Orthodox, within
Byzantium's unfallen walls.
Troy is Kyoto: each of its temple columns is
a forest, its smoke bites into ozone like a spear.
The present has infected all our pasts
and we're already sick
with futures we can't cure.
What is that virus in your voice
that waits like all these cities' dose of Troy?

The Old High Light

> *Childe Herbert tae thi Yeats' Tower came,*
> *thi Tower wiz shut, sae Bill went hame.*

1

In the curt morning of my thirty-ninth year
my mother sent me a compass from Dalvey's
as if to enquire if I had lost my way.
She was in Donegal at the time, her dear
gift in North Shields, while friends of mine invaded
the strongholds of those former Picts
which flank the River Tay, adopting the subjects
and even the language I've deployed in screeds
I know now take too long for you to read.

The previous year I'd lain upon my bed,
low in the Old High Light, our square white tower
that looks across the Tyne towards Arbeia,
having received a wine-rack – and the bell
rang, but I couldn't raise myself to answer,
and watched out the window as she went away,
some woman, pausing at the steps to the quay.
Something about her reluctance to leave increased
my sense of missing an opportunity.

And thirty-nine's as far as I could stare
when I was a kid: the hinge, the logan-stone
I still can't see my happy way beyond.

So yet again I lift my ice-pick to
the half-solid pools of my intelligence
and take five minutes to hook the small word 'quince',
and let the river drift on by below
its casing. Fish press their Orbison eyes against
that pane so glancingly, so close, then pass:
I chuck my father's face back through the glass.
What is the Scots word I once knew for 'throw'
that's neither 'lob' nor 'hoy' nor in my mouth?

And if I were in those lost Perthshire towns
where countless grannies' cooling tablet basks,
where the ancient lairds make compasses and flasks;
and if I were in deep in my own country, down
in Fortingall or Ballater, Fingask;
and if I were on the street of Callendar
where my father and John Fernie crawled from bar
to bar, then at the end of every street,
at each edge, I'd see my mother, small as limits.

   2

The boats bunch in the Gut,
the wood-walled harbour underneath
my window, and I read
the letters PHAETON LOC
painted white where one used to be tied,
as though commanding that tired charioteer.

And sometimes the sunlight seems
to pause, gazing on the scrim
of timber, reeds, stained polystyrene.
Fishermen must rely upon
one-sided arguments with
their God and governments.

Diesel like His dissolving covenant
leaks out into the estuary.
The boats digest the sea
and leave the scraped-out rims
of plaice and cod sticking to the roads
like the soles from legionaries' boots.

3

The tower was never my idea –
a house that's painted ivory
above a fading industry
would tend to make a poet wary.
but standing over rivers, both
the Tay and Tyne, and staring past
their far shores, always facing south,
their estuaries' lenses, east:
this seems to be my true perspective.
Not for the capitals that lie
past South Shields or the hills of Fife
but for those other troubling cities
not occupied so much by loss,
that necessary verb of change,
as by the fear of loss's echoes –
first the loss of how to gauge
the value of each voice that dies:
antrin story, common soul,
each document that signifies
that here was an attempt at home.

I see I've grown the opposite
to verse that's now predominant:
its tone that briefly names those sites
which pin us to the lyric moment;
that finds them functioning within
the loving body and a State
which cannot love us; that confines
all sins but ours within our hates.
But though we're sure that everything
apart from our unproven selves
must die, within these deft machines
there sits, autonomous as nerves,
a second echo: how we shift
from gaping child to jittered ape,
that loss that acts like it's a gift
the way that myths once handled rape.

This Old High Light is not so tall
that I can see, beyond the hooves
of Pushkin's horse, a land that exiles
us equally from fears and loves.

The day I dragged my family
from Galway Town to Ballylee
the wrens were wringing song from trees
but Yeats's tower was closed to me,
the way that stronghold of the Trojans
stays unassailed by most
and poetry's a mess of slogans
selling poignancy to ghosts.
And so I ought to meditate
in my wee Babel, but you've heard
about Byzantium's best robot,
the one the bishop saw, the bird?
Though we digest then censor myth
the third of loss's echoes is
the poem, like a metal fish,
as useless as it makes the dish.

4

Gulls float by my window
in the gloaming,
their left oxter and their underside of wing
a bricky blood-smeared tone.

The river's smoothing down
to those fine hair lines
a woman's thigh gets when she bends:
a launch just strokes against them as it goes.

5

Ulysses tried to dodge the draft
by sowing salt and acting saft:
said Palamedes, 'Drap his son
afore the plough: he stops, we've won.'
When Palamedes made up dice
randomness became a vice,
before this deities had meant
disasters we call accidents.
Then after he'd invented chance
he built a lighthouse: let flame glance
and rock and sandbank can replace
the drowning mouth, Poseidon's face.
Small wonder that Ulysses got
the Cretan framed: he'd found the plot.

6

Angel of wax and wicks,
angel of coal and timber and reflectors,
angel of gas and light houses,
angel of the electrics, of the racks
of unwatched videos of *Football Italia*,
of the ancient vinyl, of the book-crusted study,
angel of the plaster *kouros'* head,
of the *genii cucullati*,
angel of the smooth and sleeping pow of the child
and the tangling hair of the wife,
guard a house.

Angel of the in breath and the out,
angel of the other shore,
angel of the spine's blade and the belly's globe,
of the foot's bubbling sole,
angel of decapitation, angel of the darkened
inner chambers washed by unsuccessful tides,
watcher of *duende*'s flowing and its ebb,
angel who can fill with darkness,
angel who can empty light,
angel of the breath which touches a page,
keep that space.

Angel of ink and pixel,
angel who watches carbon think,
angel of the grain of paper, of its water marks,
angel of its loaves and fishes,
angel of the crumbs that dictionaries gather,
of the bones that no one's writing down,
angel of the shopping list, the post-it note, the envelope's back,
angel of the lecture note, the borrowed notes, the crib,
angel of the lecturer, the lawyer and the hack,
hermetic angel of the soundbite, the slogan and the verse,
hold a word.

Angel of petrol and rubber,
angel of the autobahn, the strada and the M6,
angel of motorway services pasta and the foreshortened crawler lane,
angel of the Fiat, gesture of all making,
spirit of the Punto, the point we try to reach,

the bridge we try to cross, of indication,
angel of the Picassoan silence before journeys,
angel of the soundtrack that we match to landscapes,
angel of the variable reception of Radio 3,
bring us home,
bring us all home.

NOTE: 'The duende, then, is a power, not a work; it is a struggle, not a thought.
I have heard an old maestro of the guitar say, "The duende is not in the throat;
the duende climbs up inside you, from the soles of the feet." ' – LORCA

Iron Carp
(Made in 1750 by Miochin Munetsugu)

With hinges on his fins, and scales
that are not merely like, but are armour,
more Pre-Raphaelite than samurai,
he swims in the Laing Gallery.

Tangy brown with scurf marks,
he swims as though his usual
medium was not this glass ark
but rust and cooking oil.

Hugely lugubrious
with his glazed-out glimpse,
his three-day eyes and bomb-head pout,
he looks as though you just called him

a dirty name. If he wasn't Japanese
he'd be an Isambard.
He looks like he can swim
up a river of broken glass.

If he thrashed out of this case
to crack the Victorian tiles,
he'd gasp repeatedly like a car does
when it tries to start, and fails.

The Birds

1

You call them gulls
we caad thum maas
oot whaur thi language sterts
tae flicker atween
fret and haar

and thir furthir-oot nemms
flurry i thi mooth
i thi wey they suddenly
fill thi sky wi crehs:
Black-backit, Great and Lesser, Herrin, Tern.

When thi fleets
of Fifies and Zulus
and aa thi fisher lassies
follaeit thi shoals tae Shields,
whit did they creh thi gulls?

2

In thi auld photies ye see thum
stude by thi ile-black barrels
thir peenies gleamin wi
thi glit o thairms,
thir herr in heidscarves, nearly Muslim,

and thir een and smiles
owre quick fur thi exposure,
thi semm as those Eh saw
in Buckie and thi Broch,
in Peterheid and Aiberdeen.

Eh watch meh dochter,
boarn in thi Granite City, slawly
shuft hir plumage, be
mair Geordie nor thi quine
Eh thocht she wad become.

3

Hoo could ye fool a gull?
They gee ye thon sidelins
glisk o yella
tae mind ye by
then shit oan yir car.

Ut's anely when thi boats come in
prime wi cod an praans,
haddies, skate and plaice,
and gang by thi herbour
straicht til thi ice facktry

that aa thi roofs ur aa at wance
a hoatch o maas,
a misery of beaks,
and aa thi air adrift
wi shadows oan a stervir.

4

They fecht ilk ither fur
thon guano-skliddy throne:
thi orb of oak aa cleidit in leid
that sits oan thi cupola o
thi Auld Heich Licht

nae suner hiz wan wrapped
uts webbit feet aboot ut
than anither's flappan at uts heid:
they're mair lyk love
nor ony ither burd.

They staund oan roofs
an rails an sheds:
thi maas aa mum
thi gulls aa gleg,
and waatch thi catch come in.

---

fret (Geordie), *haar* (Scots): sea-mist; *creh:* call, name; *Fifies, Zulus:* types of Scottish fishing boats; *peenies:* aprons; *glit:* slime; *thairms:* guts; *een:* eyes; *thi Broch:* Fraserburgh; *thi Granite City:* Aberdeen; *quine:* young woman (in the North-East of Scotland); *sidelins:* sidelong; *glisk:* glimpse, flash; *mind:* remember; *hoatch:* continually moving crowd; *stervir:* fast; *cleidit:* wrapped; *leid:* lead (also language); *gleg:* eager.

The Harvest in March

The drive from Elgin to the hospital
had no tree felled across the way, no snow,
instead the March light opened our road east,
back from the blue beyond of Bennachie.
It cast itself across the stubbled parks,
and hours of sun seemed left in Aberdeen,
and so we walked out for the last time as
a couple. In the chipper you announced
'It's coming,' and you squatted, scaring both
me and the granite wifies serving me.

Twelve hours gave you your own geography:
a canal with a head stuck in it, so
they reached for forcing drugs, the opening knife,
and that domestic-looking suction plug
which pulled a girl out like a plum, still on
her stalk, since in the country inside you
it's always autumn. Wheeched her wheezing off
to thread her little nostrils with those tubes
that siphon out the faeces. Which looked like
she was being stitched onto our loud world.

And when I brought her back they'd stitched you too:
you chatted with the surgeon as he finished
your perineum like a trout fly, and
I handed you our daughter in a towel.

Hedge School

I'm sitting outside on our red plastic stool,
listening to the dunnock on the old slum-slope
from here down to the Fish Quay, now a hedge
of rosehip, bramble, snowberry and elder.
I'm listening to the long hum of engines
that spreads across the stillness of the river
as though we could hear the turbines that drive the water in
and out. The clouds have slid down to the rim of things
and the sun is blintering the scratched-lens sky.

My head drifts back to dinosaurs, their reptile layer
that moves below our lying consciousness:
and my pan of thought is claiming it relates
to the sharp Gaelic of this hedge-sparrow's notes.
Language was very like that for millions of years
till we invented the thought that we thought of it. Or so
it says. This song with its perfect pitch at things
for a moment is a remnant of how those dragons spoke.

Gulls yap and a bluetit sends out its same test signal.
My head is permitted to drift in the spring heat.

My daughter is singing in her upstairs room,
the window's open just enough to lose the words
as though I were some further species
that listens to the fossil of a verb.

The Wooden Doll

'...this curious belief that every human being possessed an inanimate stocheion, *a second repository of his physical and spiritual essence, was widely held in tenth-century Byzantium.'*

JOHN JULIUS NORWICH,
Byzantium: The Apogee

Fishwife with your shouldered creel,
bust outside this watchtower bar,
sister to the south shore's smuggler, Dolly Peel,
inhaler of *The Waterfront*'s lard
that can convert a haddock into gold:
hear the prayers of smart-arse incomers.

Gazer up the river to the listless cranes
and a random sail; the white Byzantine gilt
of sun receding like a tide;
over Clifford's Fort that seems to be rebuilt
as a dry-docked boat; Taylor's ice-strewn display
of catches you never carried:

glaucous duck-nosed sturgeon,
grapple-fingered gurnard,
gelid pats of delicious monkfish.
You see the white spectacle band
between the black bream's eyes;
the blood-pink lenses of red mullet.

Matrushka of the Tyne,
your other selves recede in time:
before you and below you sits
The Prince of Wales with its
red-dressed iron girl, who stands
for all the figureheads without arms
reduced to stumps before her,
hacked by fishermen and sailors
for wood charms for each voyage.
Her hieratic black hair coils
like archaic Kore in the Acropolis,
that beginning smile replaced by this
resolute unblinking pout against
the hillside's thirty-foot wave.

Luck gets bigger the further back
we look for it, till we hit the time before
the birth of chance, when things could only occur,
good or bad, because you'd paddled
in something's entrails or the idol
told you what was not yet here.

Gutter of the herring, front lass for the brewer,
Palladium of the Gut where boats grow fewer,
stocheion of the families who die away,
give from that creel to those who've come to stay.

Condowan

1

Sit Jackie in the sun
that's come so soon for March,
a thing you couldn't do
a month ago.

He'd be gone to gauge the catch
come in from half a fleet
(the rest is cheaper brought
by rail from Peterheid).

Or he'd be in the shed
like a neater North Sea floor
full of things that will never
go to sea but could:

creels no lobster would
have the chance to drown in,
one the length of an eel
for his step of a garden.

Our broken fence's planks
became his shelves
with a slick of gloss
carried on from previous –

his narrative of salvage
since retirement, since
the loss of his lass,
the Aiberdeenie wife.

She's merging slowly with
his first boat, *Condowan*,
bought in my North East:
the portrait breasts his wall.

My father and my daughter
visit while I watch
him witnessing the morning,
the tumour growing like roe.

The same tides and
their different boats,
the same sun and
its different March.

His son sits by him
more and more,
his own boat in the harbour
just below.

2

There's a deid man lyin up thi stairs
i thi hoose next door tae oors,
drinkin in his dochters' tears
lyk Easter's brichtest flooers.

Thi river's mintin scales frae thi sun,
thi dunnock's in thi bush,
and singin at thi blue firth's run
as quick as ony thrush.

Thi boats huv left thi herbour fur
thi blur o sea and sky:
few gulls, nae cloods, some heat i thi air –
a caller day tae die.

Sune Jackie's aff tae sea fur guid
in a fishin boat o seasoned wuid.

Shields Ferry

1

Standing above or standing upon the ferry, I watch
it cross between the two Shields of the Tyne, carrying
the useful folk I cannot join, having no purpose to go south
or north, except the force of memory, that at its most compressed
becomes the memory of reading. Standing above the river
in the study of my tower, my chalky High Light house,
I watch the ferry slide like a slowed-down hockey puck
across the ice of a demolished Dundee rink. Standing upon it
I remember through my feet the sway of the discontinued Fifies,
the ferries across the Tay before I was five,
before the road bridge was built in Dundee.
In each case I'm useless, displaced and thinking of the past,
and the poets who stood or thought of standing or remembered
crossing on ferries between our clear diurnal moments,
as though the transit was a jar of river water, held up
to check the progress of the sunlight through its sediment.

2

And looking from the High Light it seems there is
a breath in the water, making the light live:
breath of the water and breath on the water,
pulse of the waves and pulse through the waves.
The river shifts its shimmer and drifts its shades
      like clouds, like continents,
till the memory of keel-trails is bluer than
the memory of tides. Sparks glit in impacts like rain,
and sunlit patches travel upstream like shoulders,
like swimmers doing the butterfly, like children's drawn gulls
or the backs of skates, the curved, punning backs of rays.
The light goes athwart it too, skinkles up to edges, hulls and piers,
their dark bands, it catches channels' openings, partings made
by the ferries departing and arriving constantly.
A little smoke blows across these opposites of shadows
      and the sky opens some more.

3

This is where the river says 'S'
and the sun slathers a blindness down it
like the opposite of ink:
the ferry's like one of those pads
for pressing ink into the metal of a typeset page,
it's like a moon or the lost dot
of a little letter 'i', traversing the river's huge capital;
it's the small satellite of the word 'crosSing';
it's the boustrophedon eye that, reading, can make sense,
both forwards and backwards, of the fact
that the river is printing out the sky.

4

I look across to South Shields where Barry had his office,
MacSweeney of the Shields *Gazette*, ranter of the tides,
dandy faller down the stairs of prosody, caster out of demons who
found forty more, clinking in the cellars of the Roman fort,
singer of the black foam anthems of beaujolais and punk,
celebrant of the pearl-pure palate of Northumbria, audible across
the river, but cleft by the Wall; hearer of the northern measure,
its sinews and its seizures drawn from between the teeth
of Bunting and MacDiarmid like whisky bottles and pipestems.

5

It's that time of day when the sun lays a fat smear of light
                              upon the Tyne
and the smoke drifts through it from down by the ferry dock
where there's a yard that's never working, and the ferry is dark:
the kernodge or dabber pushing ink into a plate. In Grasmere
                              I watched
a man print me a Bank of Scotland eighteenth-century pound note,
and now the Tyne is steel-lined copper: the people parade below me
with prams and dogs, and the gulls that blink my window feel more
                              like passers-by
than the strollers in the sunlight, the rushers to the ferry.
        Earlier I could look beyond the bend,
to where the huge container ship with 'HUAL' on its side
was visible over the rooftops like an apartment block, but now the sun
won't let me see. The guy working on the scaffolding at the foot
of the other High Light is missing, the man who has to work
with his back to the best view in Tyneside, but I'm not missing:

I'm here and leaning over to see the sharpness of the gull-shadows
and the masts on the dock, and the big blue that's dwarfing
the clouds retreating inland. It looks as though steam is rising
                                                   from the water
as the sun beats it into money.

6

I was too early for the ferry and had to have a half
of Guinness in *The Chain Locker* where the folk discussed their dogs
for half an hour, until I didn't know the breed they'd bought
but understood their need for such companionship:
the something that is always with you knowingly;
the being witnessed being kind or so you think I thought
as I went down the blue and iron jetty to *The Shieldsman*.
Everyone was sitting in the brown formica-panelled space
in the flicker and the swaw and the sick smell of diesel,
and I walked past then returned to the man by the door
with a Christmas card upon his small white shelf,
and got my ticket. Some boys with shaven heads
dashed out on deck to cling to the bars like frozen apes
and I followed to look down at the churning
that held us to the jetty, the making of brown momentary leaves,
their big rhubarb veins that vanished in the swill of froth;
and as we pulled away in the afternoon light
I looked at the empty docks beside us, their black edges holding
bleak water, their greasy apparentness, then I looked up
at the lighthouses, the high towers like old teeth,
and at the Fish Quay thrang for once with boats
and saw how quickly we were moving away from the mouth
which felt like something withdrawing from a child.

7

I was both there on the ferry and up
in the study I could see receding;
I was thinking about Morgan, how I love him
and I never said, the him I only know through words:
his work is my work's master.
What's to be said beyond
the dialogue of reading? Time spent
with each other's books, alive
only through this extra sense, the other as text.

What's left but what I do not have
with any of my fellow-travellers here:
that, divorced from all acknowledgement,
our words share the vital talk of family,
our ink's one blood.
            The link, like blood
is stronger than our likes and loathings:
it survives us strangely, is intimate
across the centuries, is better than meetings;
it touches us closer than wealth or fame,
sustains us through the dying of our name.

8

This is the contact brought to anyone, clumsy
as a trod-on foot and the hand clutching
for balance, asking for the momentary carrying,
the wet hand's clasp in the spray that I know now
is Whitman's, the grain of that palm, its softened
calluses, is what I extend to you, passing through
the pages on your way to memory
and crossing to the other shore you know it's me.

For who can a book hope to be loved by
but passengers? Who could it marry but
that same inconstant you, a reader,
dearer than you think. For you we'd leave
our ink relations instantly, as you do always,
rightly turning to flesh at anyone's request,
            abandoning the page.

9

There is a light discovered in the water
as you lean towards it, in its first fathom,
its man-allowing measure, its holding of
a woman or a kicking child above the darkness
for a time, that more variable unit.
This is the same light seen by thousands as
they cross and have crossed, looking out
from magazines and over briefcases and bags.
To the men who check their nets at Shields,
that light's familiar as the timber whorls below their feet
before they trawl the squadrons, silver in

the way we think of matinee screens, the same
curl of smoke across things from their engines.
The same light seen by gutting girls, by the men
in cork-pad jackets, whose lifeboat clunks
among the sink of bodies, looking through
their swirling hair for any hand
still quick enough to grip.

                     This is the light
seen by the man upon the ferry to Manhattan;
by Lou Reed and Harvey Keitel, going home to Brooklyn
with cigars between their teeth; this is the ferry
which must traverse the main street of Amherst;
which then passes beneath the bridge upon the Neva
where there's a polar bear in a flat cap leaning over;
it goes doon the waater past Greenock, past Davidson
and B.V. Thomson and Sydney Graham, all sharing
a silver flask among the rope coils of the docks;
it goes past Tagore on board his houseboat,
zamindar of the hush of afternoon, light verdurous
and spooling on the Padma.

10

                     There is a light
the value of which it's hard to measure,
just as it's hard to tell if the weight of a memory
is more than the weight of an action: it fills the Tyne
with the bodies of the poets, it drapes it with sunset
as it flows on downstream of the bones and soap,
the sawdust, stubs and ashes, all the spit it can hold.

The evening edition is pouring from the presses of the hills:
it rushes out past South Shields as it must, as it must pass
North Shields too, from the tower's top and from the ferry's deck
I watch it wash away the poets not the verse, shrouding them
in light as good as frets and the north pier's knell.

2

WANDERT

'The apprenticeship,' he declared eagerly, sitting out forward
'The apprenticeship, you know, is twenty years.'

PAUL DURCAN

Slow Animals Crossing

Lemurs somehow, at that lilt of the road
up and sideways at the trees, stooping through
the farmyard on the way to Derrybeg.
Surely there are slower creatures who could cross:
turtles with their solemn wiping gait
or sloths who swim as though to sink
is no disgrace, such aqualungs of air would be
trapped among their matted spider hair.
I think of water since that night was full of it
and white frogs leapt into my lights
like chewing gum attempting
to free itself from tarmac. And I think of lemurs
whenever I see that sign with its red letters
because of the night, and the story
of the three men walking home, and the man
on the left said 'goodnight' to someone, and
the man on the right, 'goodnight' to someone else
and the man in the middle asked who
were they talking to? And one had seen a man
and one had seen a woman, and both
described the third man's parents, turning off
at the road to the graveyard. And when I thought
of lemurs I'd forgotten they were named
for the Latin word for spirits, and I only saw,
crawling slowly in my mind across the night road
back to my parents' house and my daughter,
the bandit eyes and banded tails and soft grey backs
and the white hands of lemurs, delicately placed
upon the twist and the shrug of the road.

Reversion

They say they came from Donegal,
the parents of poet and tragedian William 'Topaz' McGonagall.
'Dundee' and 'Dun na nGall' – you might contend
they were as taken by words' beginnings as he was with their ends,
for, despite his atrocious sense of timing,
he never could quite dispense with the harmony of rhyming.

But no matter how I search among his literary roots
I can find no precedent for his always adding, in the clinching
    second line, a supernumerary foot.
An innovation seized upon by Ogden Nash,
who found the greater the irony in this delay, the greater the
    eventual return in cash.

And irony is certainly among my conclusions
unless I'm oversensitive to what I take as Fate's allusions:
it would justify the way my Dad
has now retired to Donegal, so I must visit the homeground of verse
    before it got so very bad.
A County most marvellous to be seen
with its bogs and its shrubberies and its rocks the shape of giant
    peas and beans.

Its mountain ranges are both large and fair:
while Muckish roots in peat, Errigal tends to snuff the air.
And if there were a place I'd like them to row my coffin
it would be into the shine of waters west past Gola and Inishboffin.

A hard County to farm and a harder one to leave,
but it's how it produced our tone-deaf Bard that it's hardest to believe:
this Ithaca is thick with music all the livelong day
whereas the thickness of McGonagall shines forth in his every
    earnest lay.

I'd ask that master of the Irish Cathal Ó Searcaigh
if I wasn't sure he'd strike me with a spade for the ignorance of
    this malarkey.
And though some like to look on Dundee
and claim its grimness leads inexorably to dreadful poetry,

I'm more inclined in the end to suppose
that McGonagall's guff is somehow leavened enough by the genius
        hereabouts to give birth to
        the only bad poet the whole world knows.

Our Lady of Brinlack

Our Lady in the window of dead Nancy's home
turns her small blue back upon
the hills beyond Gweedore
and the islands, open to this summer's ocean, low –
their houses no one lives in
but receives a grant to paint,
beaches you could almost swim to for a dare.

She spreads her chipped bone hands and doesn't look
away from Brinlack upon
the shoulder of the Foreland.
She doesn't see dead Conol's gable opposite
or where we've sat for four years now
in Liam Ferry's bungalow
and paid her just one visit.

She concentrates on sheltering this cornered space
as it disintegrates into
a daughter's cupboard
and some nieces' sometimes vivid memories.
She doesn't have to look
like others here to where
the sun will tear air's membranes and go down.

The Westering Eye

In the time it takes to fetch a camera
the powder-brush burst of an orange cloud
has gone like a car-chasing collie for
the horizon, while the greying
purple streaks continue
echoing the islands as they rear against
the glitter passing further out.

There's no one else in sight to witness
what film's too slow to catch:
shifts in something like a proof
while something like a nation shifts
on its seats, secure before its sets,
their necessary imitation of
a passion it must fork and churn and stack.

Just my father leaning in the doorway
waiting for the green flash as
the sun goes through the water,
as they used to claim would happen
in the seas by Singapore.
The flash he doesn't quite believe in
in a ceremony that he does,

prepared as he is to cross himself
at the descent of light
and the raising of colours that denote
some limitations: that time
must curve, forget, and start again.
The flaming of a kind of sword
that lets us all go on.

Poisoned Glen

In the tea-room of the Lakeside Centre at Dunlewey
or the Ionad Cois Locha at Dun Luiche
I find myself reaching for the teapot as if I meant it
yet again aspiring to the condition of adulthood
as you do as a child, convinced
the effortless others about you mean it –
the tall man improbably out with his well-dyed mother;
the father with the three orange kids,
correct amount of hair and wife same age as him;
all the comfortingly comfortable citizens around
with their small glasses of Fanta filled to the brim;
even the ducks out the window,
orating briefly on the slithery stone
in the brook which has just started turning white
as though blooming with Dettol –
as though they all could mean it.
My mother and my daughter return from the toilet
and, resuming our deep-fried repast
of whiting and chicken nuggets, we look out
towards the speckled rounded thrush breast walls
of the Poisoned Glen
one letter away in the Irish, so they say,
from being the Glen of Heaven.

Ecumenical Couplets
(for Mary O'Malley)

I drive Dad's Rover with a gentle push
through students possibly perfecting Irish

in flirtatious evening strings along the gravel
that runs across the bog back from Chapel.

Conscious as an absentee from Mass
that I am like bog-cotton or a ghost

attempting to heave through their living bones
and tissue to a place I'm not at home.

Although the Calvinist in me can't stick
it's too late to protest I'm Catholic.

Walking Home at Midnight

There are places you will never be at home
and times when you should know it
or go wrong somewhere
under where you think.

For me it's Saturday night
walking with my father back
from the *Heights*
with the moon a low glow in the dark,

red as a curling lump of turf
in the houses they preserve
to show how things were done
in the days before folk thought of coming home.

The dry balanced walls of huge hailstone boulders
are nearly visible,
each rock possessing just enough edge
not to roll, to withstand all gales,

most enclosing still
a small crop of darkness:
we step off the gravel
and they're reaped by car headlights.

The puffball houses bloat at us,
the newer ranchalows beside
the old rows
of cottage byre and shed

leaning on each other like
the sections of an opened telescope
put down after checking the light
on Inishirrer's little cape.

We're thinking of the small hours walk
when he met the groaning float of a face
coming up the hill from *Jack's*,
how it followed him back to his house,

a dim unknown man he said goodnight to,
just as he'd greet old Conol (who
spoke to no one till he died) –
then woke to find a white-faced horse outside.

There are places you can witness but not live
because they ask you for a whole
acceptance that you cannot give.
By showing this, they point you home.

* * *

...Troy, founded by Cretans on the advice of Sminthian Apollo
after an assault by rodents, sminthos meaning 'mouse'.
Troy of the walls built by Poseidon and the cowboy work
of Aeacus, easily breached by his son Telamon.

Troy of the golden veil of dragon-redeemed Hesione,
who, after Heracles had slaughtered most of the sons
of Laomedon, saved the last from the slave-block,
and he was renamed Priam.
                    Troy of the porpoise-boned
and legless Palladium, possibly fallen from Heaven;
stolen by Odysseus and Diomedes (the Ithacan bound
to stop him stabbing his pal and taking all the credit);
Troy of the wooden copy that ended up in Rome.

Troy of the thumos, the organ Homer tells us
tells men what to feel, no longer to be found
in the spear-dagged abdomen of Turnus of Latium.

Troy of the induced abdication of Romulus Augustulus,
which beats being dashed from a tower by Neoptolemus
or maybe good old Odysseus, like Hector's infant son...

The Bees
(for Debbie)

Two bees that come to me as I read,
busy on the beach at Georgioupoulis,
you sitting by the nearby pool. Two bees
for the pairing of parts that make up a woman:
breasts, mouths, her brain's two hemispheres.

Each different, so the singleton that's male
can digest the thyme-sweet tang of their message.
The first buff-tailed, fond of the feet of women;
the second black and urgent, a pulse of tar
in the glowing shadow of my water bottle.

Reminders that the moments full of words will slip,
the actions fail to grip our memories,
like how when driving back from Falcarragh
I thought I'd caught a dry leaf blowing in the back,
crackling at the edges of my turning eyes,

then saw as I crossed the boggy moor below Errigal
that I had carried from its tribe one bee,
one tiny Amazon rattling between back windows.
And I thought of you, your name, your busyness,
and felt that touch of danger at a sting.

I wound the windows down by touching two buttons
and the bee left somewhere by the turning for
Dunlewey, to forage in strange flowers and
to carry pollen far from home.
                              I rise in Crete
each time: once to come to you, and once to write.

Ormos Almirou

'Water and sunlight contain all the colours
And suspend between Inishbofin and me
The otter, and thus we meet...'
MICHAEL LONGLEY

Bobbing with my daughter in the Cretan waves,
their salt-snort window like slugging jade
that neither opens nor closes on the view beneath:
a desert of wrinkles that the sea composes
then wipes out, to show her sway over days,

I glance sideways as she rises in her ruffled swimsuit,
tries to be a crest that the lip doesn't need,
but it's higher than her hair: she arcs with its roll
and is contained for a moment, like
Longley's otter in the Mayo swell, is borne

facing out through its pane till she breaches in light.

Dancing in the Waves

All morning Vassili has
been fighting with the waves,
carting sun-beds and replanting parasols.

All night they have been washing
at his little strip of beach,
deafening lilos, eroding his livelihood.

The light was on late in his caravan-hut
as he contemplated stars:
how much cloud obscures his summer's wage.

For weeks the flow was soothing
and the faces went in rhythms,
with the few he remembered from last year.

And only the occasional
extravagant vagrant drunk
to be lifted from his stretch of sand like tar.

Each night, his hair brushed smooth,
he'd sit in his sister's taverna
accepting beers and waving at the likes of us.

Today is like those stories
when the Fianna visit Greece
disrupting all the placid folk with spit.

Either Lir has sent his horses
or Poseidon's stirred his trident:
three lines of laziness reduced to one long strip.

Vassili and his mallet
transplant all the umbrellas,
he's stomping like a bear that won't get wet.

He refuses half his usual fee
and smiles upon my daughter –
then roars out at his wife for quicker help.

Some children dance defiance
in the uncertainty of shallows,
their parents hanging by with lifeboat smiles.

A staggered soul emerges
with jelly tree-trunk legs:
a Zorro Z of reed upon her flank.

My family is bobbing
in colossal pea-green troughs.
They vanish, leap and shriek, and won't come in.

And now and then the clear tone
of the mallet of Hephaestus
is sounding out like flint along the sand.

3

INSTANTINOPLE

'...everyone is in a different era...'

MIKHAIL AIZENBERG

In Transcript

I try deciphering Cyrillic
shuffling toward Passport Control
but it's beyond me – brute-idyllic:
I thought the low roof made of rolls
of carpet but it's actually
brass rounds, so archaeologically
the seventies I feel at home
until Unsmiling Girl intones,
'Moment.' My passport and this woman
then vanish through an unmarked door.
I'm staring at the case-tracked floor
while, for her Harry Palmer "moment",
in which I too get mistranscribed,
my visa is that of a spy.

Spring Hits Leningradskiy Prospekt

Alyosha's tall with lifeless hair
and a parallel scar to his nose groove,
he's very young with a grimy white car.
There's no kerb between the pave-

ment and the road. Men shake hands till
he bumps against their barrier,
police stop you once you're through.
The sun's so sudden it all looks filthy.

He starts becoming 'Alex' as
he drives too fast in and out of lanes
and smoking to remember English names
and scorching down *Leningradskiy prospekt.*

There's a jam at the Garden Ring
because they've half-built an eight-lane bridge
and the road is full of people bringing
everything out to their dachas

including the fridge. A guy in a Merc
chunders down the mud
of the central reservation. The verges
fill with heat-smitten Ladas.

Alex doesn't know what looks worse,
the pseudo-classical Stalinist blocks
or Khrushchev's pseudo-useful ones. Winters
cramp you in like springs in clocks.

Pre-revolution stuff is custard,
powder-blue; true Russian's thick-
walled, low with white edgings. Then we pass
a factory called *Bolshevik,*

which makes bars of chocolate.
Two women walk in front of it
eating great bread haloes
called *boboliy* or *bublik.*

He tells me to sniff its scented air –
I only get dry petrol, beautiful,
but the right wind will sweeten a neighbourhood:
he likes to see this smell.

Crossing the Youza

So concrete does that flow of water seem,
crossing the Youza with Sasha and Lena
is like walking across the muddle-laned
flyover over a deserted motorway.
But because we're entering the Kitay-Gorod,
the oldest, once wattle-palissaded
suburb of the Kremlin, it's still worth a huzza.

And Russian is the alphabet you see
asleep: a liquid of letters that seems to ice
at your eyes' peripheries, saying somehow
Podkolokolniy pereulok or
Under-the-bell Street, where the little shrubs
grow out of the church's brick-bare belfry
like hair out of an old man's ears.

Back down the hill someone hasn't taken down
their Christmas decorations by April.
I lean upon a lightswitch in the Bistro,
the symbol for which is a grumpy hussar,
and a suit the size of the Kitay Wall
mentions I've caused a blackout upstairs.
His body language hints Yakuza, shrugs Camorra.

But then again, why folk gesticulate
so much when ordering *kvas* and *pirozhok*
is not because all Muscovites are Mafia,
but since the Deaf School is next door.
I sip my tea-bread-beer and pasty pies
and listen to Sasha's eyebrows, the thin
iconic twist of Lena's lovely nose.

They walk me past a mighty shoebox
called the Russiya Hotel, and up a mustard
administrative street that's never had a name:
we keep on leaving order for a space
more like the wood-shanked country-looking house
that's built among these tyre-tracked sandy pends
of oil-mucked walls with pipes half dented off.

The workers lean from its windows as though
it travelled in their sleep, and they wondered where
it had ended up. We had ended up by
the side of GUM, so entered Red Square.

The Resurrection of Red

There had to be a saltire of contrails just
above the Galloway Clock. The shock of so
familiar a place – albeit now in colour
and with no tanks, no missiles on trucks
scrolling relentlessly past all our pasts,
their noses chives to St Basil's onion domes...

The guidebook babbles how Ivan fried men –
in a pan, two hundred of them; Peter's still
beheading the Streltsy regiments;
and Baranovskiy's on Basil's steps
threatening to cut his throat, but Stalin says
the Cathedral splits the march out on May Day
so it has to go. It's still here and not here,
Lermontov's vodka stopper: the air feels drunk.

Lena tells me how she laughed hysterically
on shuffling past the husk of Lenin when
she was a girl, and something childish fills me
looking at blue screens hanging from GUM,
which is not colossal, square, a drabber Macey's
with cabbage tin ziggurats and no dishwashers –
it is instead baronial as Jenners.

They used to develop the giant photographs,
Marxian super-icons, in the public baths,
and Alex's favourite cathedral, Christ the Saviour,
used to be a swimming pool, *plein air*, a shroud
of steam covered it like incense in winter:
your head froze and you couldn't see who was
a foot away, floating in the apse.

If something has once existed in Moscow
then it exists forever, and will
be rebuilt or knocked down at someone's whim,
and now it's the crowd-soul-pleaser Luzhkov.
Baranovskiy, sent to prison for having taste,
hid blueprints of demolished churches
like the Khazan Cathedral now blinking out
in red neon: 'Christ is risen' – as is it.

Girls in authentic costume answer, 'Indeed,
He is risen,' from the museum restaurant,
and offer you a voucher. Lenin has
also risen outside the Moskva Hotel,
and wants me to be in a photo with him,
but I have to retreat to *Rosie O'Grady's*.

A Byzantine Education

The idea of an Irish bar in Moscow
contains the theory of a round of Guinness
costing more than my *per diem.*

GRAMMAR
One pint brings back that dark statue
of Dostoevsky: if his poor posture was a noun
then he had a very cold adjective
under his arse, something like a hatchet.

RHETORIC
Another makes me hear
the black-socked protests of my sore feet,
walking miles beneath pitiful white calves.

DIALECTIC
The third reflects the black-roomed stink
of the glassless gaping windows opposite
the displayless military uniform shop
where I'd expected action mannequins.

So much for the *trivium* of drink.

ARITHMETIC
The prints here feel they've summed up
Irishness with their views of Glamorgan.

GEOMETRY
The map of Moscow in my head is now
of circles laid in larger circles:
Kitay then Beliy then the Garden Ring,
as though within the Kremlin was some grit

ASTRONOMY
so irritating that a state arose
around it, but couldn't stop it itching –
the pearl that would become the universe.

MUSIC
At this point a blues band starts up
of fourteen year olds in Van the Man shades.

That's our *quadrivium* and all, so we sup
up: we can't afford another idea in here.

Lena leads me through the blank stylishness
of Lubyanka Metro, but we miss the last trolleybus
so we walk: either it's safe or she's fearless.

PHILOSOPHY
Moscow's a bubble blown up
to just before it bursts, and then
nailed down carefully on
Lobnoe mesto, the execution space,

for if it popped nine million people
would be saying *'Presteetya?'*
in a forest. Metaphysically speaking.

Vesodka

A honey-coloured 'high thing', like the Scott
Monument mated with Thunderbird Three,
but vaster: a boxy rocket-warren with shops
and a cinema tucked under its thrusters,
and rows of *apparatchiks*' windows
ascending between the preening statues

of Stakhanovite Ignudi. My flat
had two doors in case of decompression
or popular unrest: the outer was wood,
the inner padded leather studded into steel.
The kitchen socket 'is not in order now'
and every room had a supernumerary switch.

At night I read about the workers immured
in the walls, their moisture oozing from the sockets.
In the mornings I sipped Liptons from a china cup
traceried with half-washed-out gold
like the ones in my gran's old cabinet
and checked the courtyard trees for further leaves.

In the Alexanderskiy Gardens

In the Alexanderskiy Gardens I watch
brown birds hopping in brown dirt.
I must have missed the change of guard
for the Eternal Flame, so I just watch.

They're trucking in dark earth for the beds
and bleached-out tulip stalks in squads
like young soldiers who have vomited
and found a handkerchief from home.

A dog made out of dust and grime runs by.
The workers are taking the sacking off
the black earth heaped against the Kremlin Walls.
The tulips have wounds growing within them.

The guards in red-rimmed lunar hats advance
balancing their rifles on their white-gloved hands.
At the brim of every goosestep they delay –
and we have all left time. At each such sway

rifles float inches from shoulders, toes are gliders;
at every instant they delay the spring
will last forever. Brown birds hop
in the new dirt and bathe in hose-water –

sparrows, not frozen after all...

Oklad

'The humorous Kremlin cathedrals and palaces'
(MISHEARD ON TOURIST TAPE)

The *oklad* feels more like my memory
the further back this poem looks:
that outline, first seen in the Armoury,
for ikons it so often lacks.
The *oklad*'s gold frills frame my absence
of early faces: dead grandparents,
their focus gone like my tape's tone
of voice, the hushed shuffling on.
Case after case I felt like falling
asleep to a lullaby of facts,
their music for life's *entre-actes*.
But this shape grips you when you're failing:
the *oklad* holds a hole, and yet
holiness fills its silhouette.

Foreign Literature

Past the Smirnoff house and over the river,
past the church where Akhmatova worshipped,
we drove down the Street of the Golden Horde
that leads to the office of *Foreign Literature*.
I faced a portrait of Yuri Gagarin
Picasso had sketched in the guts of a pigeon.
The table was piled with saucers of sweets.
The editor's the first who isn't KGB.
He was absent but three assistants and
a little mozartkugeln-filled piano
stood in. I had a ten minute talk to deliver,
but we sipped tea while I eyed the shoe-tip
of the blonde one for a blade. Out the window
some young blokes examined a hopeless blue car.

The top sub-editor was spectacle-shiny,
telling me how their circulation had eased
down steadily as the accuracy
of their translations had increased.
This was the house of the aunt of a friend
of Pushkin's, a man sent back in fragments
by the Persians: the behaviour of his wife
(unlike Pushkin's) was Greyfriars Bobby-like.
Despite these lessons in the ironies
of fidelity, an eyebrow hinted at
the unlikelihood of poetry in Scots,
while every comment on our novelists
inspired flirtation, got closely noted –
yet poets last, if loosely-anecdoted.

Once back outside in the coppery light
the lane was busy with liquor booths.
I found the Street of Old Translators,
whose ghosts fill the Church of Akhmatova.
Scrape the paint off its walls and there's poetry.
Lift the slabs and underneath there's books.
Hush the traffic and they still discuss and recite.

The Street of Old Translators

In the Street of Old Translators
the word for 'biscuit' is a verb.
Each morning we awake
translating *'Ugis! Ugis!'*
into a fresh new language.
We find we've thrown a pike in the shower
where it flaps, pink and plasticky,
with a cut in its side which resembles
a woman's lipsticked mouth.
This is the word for 'telephone'.

In the Street of Old Translators
the word for 'butterfly' means
a man in a large rigid envelope
the back of which is reindeer-hide
and the front fish-leather.
Many actual butterflies' arses
stick to the hairs. Their wings are covered
with the Glagolitic alphabet.
Their flapping propels him forwards.
He smokes a moth like a cigar.

In the Street of Old Translators
the collective mind dominates
causing five or six of us to collide
each night in scumbled tackles
on scraggy pitches of text.
We translate 'teapot' into 'learner driver'.
We translate 'pancake' into 'whore'. We say
'I bet you told her all your trees were sequoias.'
We sit with the phrase *'Pajalsta, hachoo ochin piva'*
hanging out of our trousers.

'Ugis!Ugis!': The horror! The horror!; *'Pajalsta, hachoo ochin piva'*: Please, I really
want a beer.

The Icon Rooms

(Tretyakov Gallery)

Byzantium is still falling in ditches filled
with flecks of paint from the icons on display.
It's falling from fingers long enough to hold
the *Iliad* and the Gospels in one splay.
It whirls in the void between mother and child,
in whorls in the faces of the floating saints;
in pictures they claim were painted by no one
before the world ended in a single forenoon.

Theophanes fled here, bearing brushes like keys
to that place Constantinople set outside
our clocks and within these gestures. Like a disease
preserved in blood, that virus of colours spread
to Rublev, bunching his figures in eternity's
gold blast, a storm that only the holy ride:
that fragment of a face left on a board
still breathing in the air that Christ expired.

The Vladimir Ikon, Mother of God, which Luke
supposedly did, is stroked with fragments of text
like all the books desired by other books,
still burning. Its fabrics fold like architecture,
falling; and Mary holds Him as she flakes,
and it holds her through blackening and wreck.
If it was burned away, its space would hold
the absence of this mother and this child.

At the Vorabi Hills

How rare it is to know exactly what
you want. We drive past the Tartar hat
of the State Circus, back from a crumbling college
to stop off at the Sparrow Hills.

And watch the wedding couples let off fireworks
in daylight, smoky orange flares;
the brides as perfectly made-up as the trainee
teachers in dusty classrooms, as keen.

The martial fizzles float across the trees
beneath us: we're between two ski-jumps
as though we could fly into the oval torus
of Spartak's ground mid-match, and score.

Green roofs of Politburo dachas with
their own Metro line (now open to others);
the river loops the city like a sash,
or the rings exchanged here by the Pushkins.

And lovers want to visit these hills in Spring,
shrine of that inauspicious wedding;
and fifty students asked me about the future
of socialism; and trees still sprout.

I see the Vladimir Icon painted on
a wooden egg and know I want it –
like learners and the lovestruck think I've found
how to hold the city in my hand.

The brushwork is too pretty-pretty, but
we're sure there's better in the Arbat.
En route, Gagarin's steely monument
shows hope has Dan Darevitch momentum.

Lunch Poem

It's lunchtime so we go round the back of
the Kotelnicheskaya Apartments, past
the low white and extremely bulbous
Greek Orthodox monastic embassy and
cars sunning themselves, wire meshing
shadows on their unwashed bonnets.
The doorman's feeling lazy on his torn plastic seat,
the foam and his belly both visible;
we go into the cafeteria
of a newspaper I have never read.

Somewhere in this block every decade
is held in slave-sealed rooms
like rotten-lilied movie sets from long-dead Soviet musicals,
and this is mine: light pine
panelling and powder-red upper walls,
tiny hot windows and the enormous off-centre pillar.
Surely they serve Lorne sausage and black pudding in
floury morning rolls, surely cheeseburgers and
French mustard, surely
the sixties poured sideways like a grease
and collected in corners behind this serving hatch
where two women spoon buckwheat from tupperware
and heat cheese soup.

Deep in Thomson's, D.C.
there has always been a cafeteria like this
where journos sit in mirror image to
these people –
                    Moira Anthony is there, still as
                                        demurely blonde as
Mike Sang's a
                    feckless red: he's just walked in
in a hail of freckles,
                    some of which
                                        are spotting the page
where Dudley Watkins draws Desperate Dan.

Don Paterson inks in the seventeen '*Aargh*'s, each one reflecting
these folk who eat
                and argue equably
                                and slap their kids.

The skeleton of a clock – just hands and numerals – is
attached to the wall, and the lightshade's an open oblong,
a hanging coffin, with stars frosted on its glass panels.

I eat small cow rissoles with shredded potatoes
and Alex has slab o pork. The clock in
Dandyville runs backwards, and time doesn't trickle
it fizzes like this
                        intense mineral water from
a technicolour can and, before that, Georgia,
which induces longevity.
Sasha and Lena
turn up with a bag of chocolates
in orange wrappers with this building on
and we discuss the hard-boiled icon egg,
the limbo lounge between ticks
                              where uncles arc
their long-dead spines, the hat-stand where
their astrakhan hats and fedoras hang
as though resting on clouds of camphor.

As we digest we hear
the bronchial
postprandial
            hurdie-
            gurdies
of the afterlife
begin.

The Arbat

1

To look for lathe-turned eggs, hand-finished
but not too dear, among fur hats,
faux-military helmets, burnished
hip-flasks for proletariat
piss-heads:
        dodge gender-swopped *Matryoshkiy* –
the shrinking boss-men of the Russkis
compete with basketball teams; their
composers face down our Fab Four.

Eye the wall of permitted graffiti,
grey wooden doors, intensely carved,
Georgian kebab shops.
           Grope through scarves,
red-dressed dolls, emblems of the city,
and eggs, half a hand-painted mile:
wrong image, wrong price and wrong style.

2

The hunting shops have cartoon panels:
Magoo-men shoot at deer –
we too feel pitched-at, weary,
so eat our ice-creams, and just stand
like "'village style" stunned icons,
with balloon heads, skin like bacon.

We listen to a jazz band who all
lean in a line and play:
one man smokes through a jaundiced holder,
lets his accordion sway.

Two women – poised, slim –
brush Alex as he's smoking:
the fag-end gets snagged, and
his saving smack's ignored.

Lament for Mir(akovsky)
(in the Mayakovsky Museum)

Not the shot, nor
                    the death-shout
                                    from the upper floor
not the past shattered this testa-
                            tenement, but
                                        the future;
not Maya but Mir
                    spattered this brick kop this
                                            cove
of thoughtski:
                    Miro-kovsky,
                                futuronic Lili-lover,
VladiMir StarMiGovsky,
                        Dragonfly-rabotnik,
                                            Voidoid-nymph,
your solar panel-wings plucked
                            by polystylist fingers
                                        in heat's symphonics:
not into the Pacific but
                    the apartment behind
                                        the Lubyanka
your bullets smack   '
                    that brain-panic open
                                    Kvant by *Kvant*
to the thanks of illiterate touristicals
                                gyring
                                        the vorpal vortex
the stairwell they built
                    from *Core* module
                                to be your ex-cortex
ex-
    ploring the air about
                    you, bust furniture,
                                    verse torsos,
rococomontage built
                    with Osip and Lilya Briks
                                        you polarised

84

bear, Kayakovsky
      paddling in the neuston
            of neurons,
Volodya, Volosity,
      Shchen: when
          did you become a Mysteron?

It got harder to
      receive your message,
          but it was always
about this:
      from the first time
          I Herbert Read you,
the heart composed
      from orbital heights
          the head
exploded with
      new constructions
          new flaws;
I knew you obeyed
      the opposite
          to gravity's laws.
Aizenberg's pacing
      the mausolinoleum
          in your museum,
red patches under eyes,
      Jack Daniels in
          his leather stomach;
I'm looking up
      smiling Stan Laurelly
          ("village style").
Who was the first
      of cosmonauts
          that saw Mir climb?
Who was longest
      in the craft
          though its life was brief,
his heart and bones
      expanding
          with almost-relief?

Who slept whichever way up,
                    played gapuitar,
                                        made spheres
of cabbage soup and,
                    strapped to the tread-
                                        mill of Mir
ran around
            the rimshot
                    of the sky
while the Union broke
                    up on its own
                                        re-entry?
Soloviev,
        Polyakoff,
                    Krikalev:
your new names
                now we know
                            how you're alive.

Let there be
            365
                laments for your fall
from each degree
                of griot
                        beneath your roll.
Vladimirovich
            your limbs part
                        as you burn
Iron Mandalovsky,
                Kristall is melting
                                on your return
to *Priroda*,
            Spektr is splitting from
                                you, pi-Dogstar,
crackled lab, you
                ricket-rocket,
                            you epic of our desire.

Petrovich's Handy Phrases for the Visiting Writer
(to be translated into the nearest mother tongue)

Thank you for greeting me my brother/sister.
You are a great poet. I have never
heard of you before this moment.

This powerful local liquor
looks like a sick person's urine.

Thank you for your introduction, which
focussed almost exclusively on your own work.
It is indeed a pity you are not reading tonight.

I appear to have poured soup
into this tape recorder.

Please speak more quickly: either
you were beginning to become intelligible
or I am about to black out.

It is 5.30 in the morning:
the horror! the horror!

Please stop the vehicle, I wish to emit
pressurised vomit and excreta by the roadside,
hopefully from the correct orifices.

I can assure you my publisher will be eager
to spit upon your manuscript.

Thank you for an instructive tour.
The bones in my feet are dissolving.
Please don't let me roll weakly into the forest.

Note and honest disclaimer: Petrovich is a Moscow satirist who owns a restaurant as hospitable as my hosts on this trip, the British Council. No blame can be attached to them for the experiences, many of them fictional, some of them taking place in other countries, described in this poem.

May Day

It's 5.30 in the morning, May 1st.
I'm reading through a hangover
Misha Aizenberg's canny essays,
oblique and bleak, as strong

as bread vodka in Petrovich's place,
that cartoon restaurant.
I rise, scrape from the front of my face
fuzz that remains behind it,

and eat yoghurt in the kitchen of
an old school friend, James Meek:
journalist and writer of novels
folk think *Trainspotting*-chic

but here I see are more Bulgakov
than Irvine. We're far older
than we looked last night, so drunk we talked of
writing until cool-shouldered

by his lovely weary wife. The light
is clear green on morning roofs;
the May light on the other flats,
same green as the new leaves.

I listen to the courtyards' echoes,
unfussed, the way milk trembles
in fridges. Vertical flaws in the window
make the house-blocks ripple.

It's May Day in Moscow. Cars can start,
people may turn their heads.
Friends can get stockier, wispy-haired,
words may stumble on parade.

A Caucus Race

'When Ivan clambered damply up the steps at the place where
he had left his clothes in the care of the bearded man, not only
his clothes but their venerable guardian had been spirited away.
On the very spot where the heap of clothes had been there was
now a pair of check underpants, a torn Russian blouse, a candle,
a paper ikon and a box of matches.'
MIKHAIL BULGAKOV,
The Master and Margarita

The first red flags have started streaming
over *Bolshoy moskaretskiy* Bridge
as we speed under it. I'm dreaming
of a pregnant woman half-submerged
in the Moskva, her big hemisphere bared.
Sasha tries teaching me some swear-words:
'Fuck off' is *yoma yo*, and 'Whore'
is *blini*. Earlier, inside the doors
of my flat I'd found a pair of long johns
containing Ken Smith. He'd arrived
last night, lost track of Moscow time –
I thought of scratch-marks in Gogol's coffin.
We drive off down Kropotkin Street
where Bulgakov's bardie lost his wits.

Our Caucus Race – one jet-lagged poet
v. one surviving too much drink –
half-copies poor Bezdomny's exploit.
We take bets who'd be first to sink
into the river, then get followed
by Ken's car off route to the Sparrow
Hills: they don't realise that I
still have an icon egg to buy.
We've also misled Sasha's director
who gets out to look at still more brides –
I grab an ovoid virgin n child.
Back on the road I doze, erect a
cathedral in each collarbone
of my woman wading through the foam.

I'm watching cigarettes that hither
and thither on the new tarmac
of *Mechurynski prospekt*, they glitter
like silver birches. In Spartak's
stadium, half-dream replaces turf with
linoleum and the team's swopped for a surfeit
of old women from my childhood: where
the goalposts should be are electric fires.
Behind grey walls, between grey lampposts,
the silver birches line the road.
And my old women are all dead
bar one. The dream's past, or almost.
A duck lands in a little pond
surrounded by more grey pylons.

Kladbische

We swig cranberry juice outside the house
of Pasternak, and break our May Day cake
while journalists ignore us. It's proposed
we don't go in just now, but visit his grave –
something in me's reluctant still to cross
that threshold. We're discussing on the way
how Russians don't preserve, they improvise,
and reinvent their nation like it's jazz.

There's small fires burning litter by
the sky-blue painted graves. We climb the hill
and Ken says voice holds everywhere you stay:
forest fires, floods, add to the core until
its tree-rings are played by the reader's eye
like a record being searched for stranger intervals.
People are eating lunch among their dead,
they're chatting as we pass like they're inside.

We tramp along the track toward his stone,
decide it's not so bad that on this trip
we spend so much time being on our own:
we're all related, and we just meet up
for death-days, like these families, we don't
have to be friends to recognise the grip
of words upon this grave. Some birds sing, glad
to have survived, if birdsong can be glad.

Church of the Transfiguration

Worship gets cramped in here, side-chapels
have sub-divided sacredness
like Moscow flats crowded with people:
this is God-and-His-Saints-shaped Space.
Their paintings gilt up every panel
where I can stoop to light a candle
for daughter and grandmother: all
eras are stationed on these walls.
The scarcity of gleams, stale incense,
the shifting styles and scales, the crowds
of saints, gold *oklad*-suits like shrouds –
you feel the prayer-locked loss of tense,
hear the praise of the cosmonaut:
God's in His *Soyuz*, looking out.

Peredelkino

Sometimes the clocks abandon you at door-
ways and you pass into a further depth,
a house in which dead relatives can thrive.

You hear them set out plates of biscuits in
the bright verandah wing, and your eyes fix
on the death-room beyond this fuss: a couch,
one lily. Back in here are fittings fit
for your byzantine ancestors: the light
hangs five dark branches from the ceiling rose –
a swirling white star – smoky cones depend.
A chipped-nose female bust at your right hand
inspects the creamy fridge that hides behind
the door out to the hall, its stairwell and
that bare room. Left of you the radio on
the sideboard's bulbed a tiny TV screen
within it that he never watched. The art's
his father's: huge nudes fold their lavish limbs
protectively round sketches of small farms.

You hear, translated, that he said he owed
everything to his father but you've moved:
your grandmothers have called you to the hall.

You stand at the stairs' foot as though about
to climb up to known bedrooms but you can't.
Hundreds of miles away a woman is
dying, the tumour growing in the place
her memories should be. This is that space,
displaced into a dacha crowded with
journalists, guides, *babushkiy*, friends,
all talking in now distant rooms as though
they're in your other country. You step back,
cross the dense border to biography
and fact. And going to the toilet, glimpse
a photo of the young man, Pasternak
as Keaton: glowing cheekbones, swollen eyes.

And then we do go up those scary stairs
and everything's the usual fodder for
the literary visitor, his boots
placed in that way they think means 'left', just where
he left them. His sparse chamber: so few books,
the sloping desk he stood at looking out
on silver birches through the same flaws in
the glass as James' flat in Moscow has.
We hear a guide recite, but he just booms –
then one old woman, one of those who sit
and witness every room in galleries,
museums – everywhere that culture clots,
stands up, exhorts him, indicates he should,
he must... I can't decipher what. It seems
that poetry is able to get lost
somewhere before translation can begin.

After, I sit beside her in the sun
of the verandah room. The samovar
is yielding heat, I'm passing her soft cheese
to spread upon her *glagol* biscuit, which
means 'verb'. I'm happy not to understand.

The Farewell to Moscow

Farewell tae thi Caledonian Club:
thir piper's blawin fit tae blub
wi a ginger beard ablow his gub –
      it's almost time;
Farewell thi rasps they bashed in a dub
      and caad reid wine.

Farewell tae thi sons o Lermontov,
hauf-Scots and hauf-Gromyko – soft!
some fiddler waants tae clear thi croft
      (pley reels, Eh mean):
it's really time Eh buggered off
      and skipped this scene.

There's fowk here fans o Dundee United
a thocht that maks ma bowels frighted:
meh poems laive them unexcited,
      these philo-Scots;
Eh'm fuhl o thochts they've no invited –
      get aff thi pot!

Farewell tae thi mannie wha huz shipped
twa dochters Scotland-wards – tae slip
thi wance we'd pass as jist a blip,
      but sendin twa:
huz Boris-whaur's-yir-troosers flipped?
      ...Eh'm best awa.

We say farewell and tak oor leave –
instead o laughin up meh sleeve,
Eh'm floored whit foreigners believe
      aboot meh hame:
when Moscow reads whit crap Eh've scrieved
      they'll feel thi same.

It's farewell tae guid Georgian grub – all
egg-breid, bean dip, fish kebab – Eh'll
miss Sasha's 'toe-ast's, champagne's bubbles,
      a dance wi Lena:
Eh'd spend meh daily dod o roubles
      jist tae remain. (Aw...)

Noo Alex speeds tae catch thi train
they caa Reid Arrow – in its wain
Durcan kept Svetska entertained
          wi in-transit screws:
Eh spend thi nicht locked in, alane –
          an needin thi loo.

Afore that ordeal, a wave o thi hat from
Alex – this byebye's near an artform:
here's Sasha rinnin doon the platform
          tae wave hersel.
This exit intae nicht feels larksome:
          Moscow, farewell.

Instantinople, third o Romes
and fourth o Troys, fur fehv deys home –
ye kerbless pend, ye ingin dome,
          ye brutal core:
ye've skelped thi place whaur Eh mak poems
          and gart it roar.

dub: puddle; *scrieved:* written; *pend:* alley; *skelped:* smacked; *gart:* made.

4

THE HORSE

You will not find new lands, not find another sea.
The city will follow you. You'll wander down
these very streets, age in these same quarters of the town,
among the same houses finally turn grey.

C.P. CAVAFY

(trs. Edmund Keeley & Philip Sherrard)

Wrists of History

When I contemplate my loved one's wrists
as they grip a succession of steering wheels –
usually those of rusted fuck-ups,
fungus-breeding leakarounds,
moving trucks and miniature rented vehicles
of the Fortunate Isles, Italy and Crete –
I reflect on their sheaths of muscle,
the almost-sharp nodules, tender as
a collarbone or half-buried gearstick;
and I think of the women drivers of antiquity,
those in whose cars I would be
a little more than willing
to be the passenger. I think of their wrists.

Lucrezia Borgia,
queen of the gorgons
who kept simmered lambs' limbs
in her Lamborghini
and played a poison dart mouth organ
as she drove: the gorgeous princess of loam
who used her car
to bury condottieri far from home.

Boudiccea who shopped in IKEA
for Swedish ice cream slops,
red caviar and loud shrouds,
for cloud nude furnishings,
dud druid sheds and rude crud,
which she would then slice in two
with the blades extruding from
her beautiful Mini Coupé.

Joan of Arc
who shared shark fritters with Petrarch
in the back of a bone-coloured Citroën
deux-chevaux, listening
to the spatter of loyal squatters' piddle
on her virginal windscreen
as they tried to put out her flames.

And Anna Akhmatova, who read
an Aga saga to her slaughtered lover
while swigging St Petersburg lager
and driving her Lada to Prague
with a pina colada
and a pavlova for later
in her proletarian glove compartment.

And I remember how Elizabeth drove us round
the tall tenements of Petersburg by night,
bumping over the rut-infested trammy lanes,
almost lost but not quite,
and I lay in the back and let the names wash over me –
Leningrad, Petrograd, Saint Pete –
until I could have pulled up in Peddie Street
at five years old,
or woken in a gutter with a strange sturgeon,
or just be being driven anywhere by you,
woman with the hundred mile wrists, so thin and strong
they bridge the continents and centuries
with one smooth twist.

The Field of Mars

*'An uncomfortable feeling: as though you're encamped
in another's time, an occupying force...'*
EVGENY REIN

The noticeboard's a grave of information,
drying, tusk-coloured tearings, stapled, gummed,
half-messages that lost their readership in
the creaking fathoms of last month, last year,
time swilling half a word: an announcement, a name,
like a glimpse of salmon in tea-coloured water.

The noticeboard's a yard of overlooking
from the Field of Mars to Elizabeth's courtyard,
a tunnel I could almost call a close.
Her stairs compress around their newel in
a dimness I half-recognise from childhood.
A ghost-dog paints your shoes with dust

each time you climb the tenement steps
to the flat of white busts and thick glasses
each holding a bullet of vodka, the view,
between bookcases leathered with Tolstoy,
of a field of revolutionary corpses buried
like old newspapers, old wrappers, old news.

To Elena Shvarts

'Slow gangs she by the drunken anes,
And lanely by the winnock sits;
Frae'r robes, atour the sunken anes,
A rooky dwamin perfume flits.'

ALEKSANDR BLOK,
translated by MacDiarmid

Elena, cleckit frae this egg Saint Pet-
ersburg, remember hoo thi sunlicht hit
oor ehs at thon daft readin? You steyed pit

in thi entrance tae thi Cameron Gallery,
stepped oot o shade tae read twa poems, then dried,
exposed as Helen oan thi waas at Troy

pintin oot Greeks tae Priam. This wiz Pushkin –
thi village no thi poet: Catherine's
wee weekend palace wi a lake plumbed in,

Tsarskoe Selo o thi Amber Room
thi Nazis stole thi waas aff – selfsame toon
whaur Anna Akhmatova's neb furst split thi gloom.

Nocturnal Helen of thi Noarth, thi poet
o Roman weemen, wierd nuns, shipwrecked parrots,
Elena, balance oan a cigarette

and gee me an X-ray o St Petersburg:
show whaur thi bullet entirt Pushkin's shrug,
Fyodor's dice he swallied lyk a dug.

Pint oot thi *Bashnya*'s hollae fingerbane:
Ivanov's tooer, fuhl oan Wednesdays
wi Silver poets lyk a needilt vein.

Seek oot fur me thi frozen Neva-slice
that hauds Rasputin's lips pucked in thi kiss
he geed Tchaikovsky as they sank thru ice.

Elena of thi paradise o rat-lairs,
thi petrifehd coup, dark beer/white rhyme, your meters
a swellachie of Moyka's roond Saint Peters-

burg, hurl me icons Eh can smuggle hame:
thae Rublev saints that flocht i thi Virgin's cream
and dinna droon but drink in scripture's dreams;

thon Silken Leddy in apartment Blok
that made MacDiarmid grab his thistlecock –
she's huggin oan a cod that smirks wi shock;

thi gran wha in thi siege of Leningrad still
preyed tae thi photie o a deid cathedral
then pinned a medal tae thi baby's cradle.

Elena, furst thing Eh saw in your toon
wiz a lassie swing a yoyo overhaund
while a streetband pleyed 'Sweet Georgia Broon':

Eh stood ootside thi Grand Hotel Europa
and waatched thi birlin o yir *mystica rosa*.

cleckit: hatched; *ehs:* eyes; *neb:* nose; *coup:* dump; *swellachie:* whirlpool; *birlin:* spinning.

The Idiot Café

The last night there I made Mark take us to
the Idiot Café. No seats were free
until the owner, hearing we were poets,
found a divan. He may have come from Glasgow.
We must have struck some note he aimed for with
      his old paperbacks and veggie blinis.

And while we were interrogated by
two German boys whose berets matched – just like
the bowlers of the Thompson twins – about
calling ourselves that name in public: 'poet',
I drifted to that morning I'd walked down
      to *Dvortsovaya naberezhnaya*,
the esplanade beside the Neva, where
I'd watched two little black boats grunt upstream
with men in yellow oilskins standing up
to steer with aluminium tiller poles:
they'd made me think of shrimping boats from Amble,
      the sheet that shields their open prow.

And as we drank dark beer a couple were
strolling on icefloes in my memory –
seen in the gallery the day before,
excited by the absence of the land.
A tall girl asked who was my favourite band –
      I said Nick Cave and she turned away.
Outside I photographed the globe above
the door, its letters bursting from Mark's head:
a moon to shine upon the broken ice
that bobbed along the Moyka, and Mark said
last year a floe with half a frozen dog
      had floated past the Idiot Café.

And sometime later we were visiting
the Horseman (I was visiting the Horse),
and I thought who was meant to ride the first,
that horse before all horses, bronze or snow-
devised? What gesture should that rider make,
      the Grand Inquisitor of Troy?

A Leningrad Confession

'I'm an idiot for you'
IGGY POP

I would inform on you
if the two of us were
in the middle of a terror:
I'd tell them what they'd think you'd do.

I'd let them into our flat
our reading/sleeping/writing room,
you'd go to God knows what
not knowing who to blame.

All our friends would board
the smallest of trains
for the fastest of journeys
through their threatening brains.

I tell you this my dear
in the gentlest of times
since other souls elsewhere
must pay for my crimes.

* * *

...*Troy of Antenor, who struck a good deal with the Greeks:*
waving a torch, tapping the Horse, and founding Venice.
Troy of the True Cross and the mantle of the Virgin,
paraded on the Theodosian Walls, which disheartened besiegers.

Troy of the Golden Horde and the savage furry crown
of Monomakh, much like the Moscow Permacircus Top;
Troy of the golden Fabergé egg that has a railway in it.
Peter's Troygrad, Great Troy of Catharine the Shopaholic;

of Robert Walton's letter before he saw the monster,
and met its maker. Troy of Lenin arriving on a train, Troy
of Knox escaping from a galley; Troy of the cold blast
and the stabbing beard; Troy of the texts of righteousness.

Troy of Geneva under spiritual siege by Catholicism;
Troy of Madrid and the navel of Spain, of the Escorial and
the claim: to rule the world with two inches of paper.

Troy of Derry that can't surrender; Troy of Dundee,
wall-less and sacked in 1547, of Dundee burned in 1651;
Troy of the Calvinist and the Pict, fictive Troy...

Laocoön in Alcalá

'...the quarrels are so unedifying, and all the Greek leaders
behave so murderously, deceitfully and shamefully, while the
Trojans by contrast behave so well, that it is obvious on whose
side the author's sympathies lay....Homer may be said, in a
sense, to have anticipated Goya, whose caricature-portraits
of the Spanish royal family were so splendidly painted that they
could have been accepted by the victims as honest likenesses.'

ROBERT GRAVES

1

First you pluck the apple from the tree,
then you eat the apple, then you throw
the apple away. And then you do it with
your other hand. Even though
we're so far north, strolling past
the brilliant grin of the refurbished
Teatro Calderón in Valladolid,
a woman shows me the method
of flamenco for my daughter.
She is as eloquent as Eve or Aphrodite
or the Empress Athenais, this
academic who laughs at forgetting her car.
We don't know it yet, but tonight
we'll eat in *El Caballo de Troya*.

2

On the last morning in Alcalá I leave
my hotel and hear a blurt of music from
the *Plaza Cervantes*. When I look
there's a series of floats that slowly
circle the square, each followed by
women and girls in full flamenco costumes.

Abruptly the music starts up again,
tinny and estranged, and for a moment
they all dance, and then as silence falls
they begin to chat again, adjusting their shawls,
following the little floats as though
compelled to dance amid their usual duties.

A column of *gigantes* marches past:
king, queen, devil, their papier-mâché heads
nodding as they go, ignoring the dancers
who start to follow. I seem to be the only
witness as they pass the old Jesuit college,
walking calmly down the middle of the street.

They look as though they're off to visit relatives
on a Sunday morning. I see Ricardo,
his beard black against the brickwork,
and go to him for his solid explanations.
His eyes are rheumy from last night's *tertulia*.
We follow them to a lane by the river.

Here the men all make their horses dance
a stiff formal volta from hoof to hoof.
Gushy-tailed and cumulus-maned,
the horses are as plush as those of Goya
which still manage to look far smarter than
the nobility on their rearing backs.

The men wear striped pants, high leather boots,
flat-crowned hats. They smoke, and toast
the women from sherry bottles, sometimes pour
a drink into the little glasses the women wear
on straps around their necks. The women dance
for a minute, then chat. The men talk on mobile phones.

Horses are tethered among the trees. Rain spots down.
The men's stirrups are huge, iron, rust-peppered,
like the masks of scolds. When the women ride
their dresses spread across the horses' backsides.
I watch two old women hold hands as they step
around the hay-coloured horseshit on the pavement.

This is not a local festival. It is the *Rocio*
where the men of Andalusia jump over
the railings of a church at first light, to be
among those who carry the Virgin in procession.
These people handle their exile as skilfully as
the men handle their horses, the women the air.

3

We drift down to the banks of the Rio Henares
to look for the ruins of the Arabic town.
The air is filled with down like horse-spittle.
We meet a photographer from the university
who's fishing with his son, and he points out
the scrap of a tower against the sandy cliffs.

The photographer now takes what I presume
to be a camera from his rucsac, but it's not,
it's a toad in a jar he's photographed and now
is releasing: a mottled, mushy apple with
almost red eyes, quite composed. Those eyes say,
'The mud is my saddle, I'll never be thrown.'

A bigger jar comes out of the son's rucksack with
a water-snake in it in an inch of river water.
The photographer offers this to me or rather
it lets me help it slither strongly through my hands
till it's swimming in the river of the morning air,
compelling me to ape the women's dance.

Its skin is moist and beady, like pearl barley.
I can tell it's thin, that it possesses a skeleton
of curved, pin-like bones, that it's maybe hungry,
maybe hungry for home. I go to the airport with
a vague white mark on me, the smell of the water
and of something not quite fish and never mammal.

Note: 'To earn the name *tertulia*, a regular time and place must be fixed – usually
in a café or bar – and participants must come prepared to speak, interrupt, contra-
dict and generally intensify the discussion. Subject-matter can range from politics,
philosophy and literature through to bullfighting and flamenco.' *Madrid: The Mini
Rough Guide.*

The Guernica Duck

The Guernica duck is shouting on the table
but nobody is listening to him.
His body is lit up like a Gurkha knife
but nobody is noticing.

Women fall and flail and thrust
but they do not throttle.
They wail and the bull wails too,
even though he is a porcelain figurine:
his tail is a fumerole,
his anus an Etna of indignation.

The horse fires cordite neighs across
the room/square: he is a newspaper blown
across your dying face. But the women
do not throttle, they do not pluck
and they do not cook
the Guernica duck.

The women have children to mourn,
husbands to lament – even the lightbulb has
a desperate sun, a bomb-burst to impersonate.
Only the duck is overlooked,
too stupid to realise that even
the bereaved must eat tomorrow.

Only the Guernica duck is shouting,
'Look at me: I'm frightened too!'
Only to him has it occurred
that he will never be forgotten.

Meeting Guernica
(after Kenneth Koch, just)

Half asleep in the Café Gijon, eating *Guernica* and meeting *Guernica*,
I have walked on my Russian-toughened feet past embassies and
  churches,
past endless rows of books about Valencian detectives and Sevillean
  bicycles.
I have cut a deep slice from a Bible full of *callos a la Madrileña*,
I have eaten forkfuls of scripture and gunbelts.
The man in the *libreria* of the Reina Sofia farted
while looking at a reproduction of Miró: when I looked at Miró
I realised that 'escargot' contained the word 'argot'
(also 'scar' 'cargo' 'Argo' 'go' and 'got' –
though I only noticed those later).
Meanwhile the girl in the Café Gijon thought I was looking at her
  bottom
when I was trying to see how people paid.
Picasso excavated a large arsehole
for the bronze woman offering a vase to *Guernica*,
but I was too embarrassed to look up it too far.

I was sleeping *Guernica* and drinking sherry,
I was drinking Coke in the gallery's cafeteria and
the Englishman there looked like Francesco Totti, *fantasista* for Roma.
I felt like asking every Spanish woman to look after me,
instead I walked through *lluvia* of their perfumes
and never met Kenneth Koch.

I was meeting *Guernica* and sleeping with St Teresa,
I was growing St Teresa's hair to pad her coffin,
I was half-asleep in the Café Gijon looking at a Hemingway lookielikie,
I was at a *tertulia* where no one spoke, where the women's heads
were very big and Kenneth Koch had just left.
Solana painted me looking depressed,
Gris painted me a guitarfish, a Jenny Haniver to sit and strum,
waiting for my mind to wake up and appreciate *Guernica*.
In St Petersburg I saw gutterfish, I saw
my publisher jump in the Neva and swim away;
in St Petersburg I saw the Finland Station but I never saw Kenneth Koch.
In Madrid I met the Spanish raindrop: it was very busy drowning
  out *Guernica*.

I was weeping *Guernica* and sleeping football,
I saw the stands of the Bernabeu Stadium full of weeping women,
I saw the dirty concrete cross of the Valley of the Fallen.
Franco cloistered all the women of Madrid in the seventeenth century
with their mobile phones and their gold, their always nubile mouths,
but the women dug tunnels and lived as rabbits.
They lived on the rabbits and as the rabbits,
they rode the rabbits to Mass every Sunday, sidesaddle
of course, their skirts covering the rabbits' scuts.
I was half-asleep in the Café Gijon as the old men pored over maps
        of old Madrid,
as they pored over maps of old Valladolid, trying to find *Guernica*.
The old men put their turtle heads together and remembered
when there were women, back in the twentieth century
when Kenneth Koch was here.

There were English people in the gallery looking at *Guernica*:
they kept saying things and there was nothing
Kenneth or I could do about it.
All the women wore black oblong glasses and had to go
back to the seventeenth century, although they were allowed
to take *Cola Cao* with them: some of them even preferred it.
All of the nudes were clothed back then, even Goya put
clothes on his nudes, even the rabbits were respectably dressed.

I was half-asleep in the Café Gijon, which is as close
as the waiters get to going to sea in their white jackets
and red epaulettes, if those things are indeed epaulettes
(if only Kenneth was here to advise me).
Elaine Feinstein would do: I heard she was in town missing *Guernica*
        too
and I missed her; I was reading about Pushkin and missing her.
I hadn't seen *Guernica* yet but I knew about the Decembrists.
Elaine and Kenneth were off somewhere eating *boquarones*
and I was drinking sherry. It was only May.
Gris was reading *tapas variadas* and Picasso was eating Paris.
I wanted to buy a *piccante chorizo* for my wife
but the symbolism was too obvious.
Neil Astley was swimming across the Baltic shouting, 'Wake up
        you idiot'
and bumping into ice floes.

But the wood was so red in the Café Gijon,
the banquettes so rosy, the narrow pillars were so
cast-iron and grooved, creamy with a century of paint,
the tables were so black and marbled and the waiters had weathered
so many storms, so much soda and sherries and *cafés solo*.

I was beginning to understand
that in the belly of the *Guernica* horse, the place
where Picasso kept his Bible, the dry room where
Kenneth wouldn't wait, where Pushkin left his boots,
where Pushkin left the boots of Pasternak too, neatly by the door,
in the womb of the horse, pierced by a lance
as a cabin is pierced by a mast,
there is an absolute calm, a total silence, a zone; there is
a *kilometre zero*.

Valladolid

'¡Ah! ¿No es cierto, ángel de amor,
que en esta apartada orilla
más pura la luna brilla
y se respira mejor?'

JOSÉ ZORRILLA,
Don Juan Tenorio

1

In the city of your childhood buildings shift
as you sleep, their known facades replaced
by painted screens: you only notice this
when the evening sun shines through the canvas.

The council is run by all your grandmothers.
At the ends of the streets dead relatives cluster.
There is a large fridge the women go in
to show off their winter clothing.

In the cafés the priests and poets sit
together, censoring the kind of volumes
the poets are not allowed to write.
The poets then revise them till

no word remains the same. The priests
ensure that no one will ever read them.
They are the poets' only audience,
and eagerly await the endless revisions.

2

There is no plastic in the city,
only bakelite: all plastic is taken
to *El Paraiso del Plastico* where
the window is filled with shabby toys.

No one builds outside the medieval walls,
yet the population continues to increase.
As there are no children, no one can tell
how this occurs. Though whenever someone leaves,

even for a day, someone else must enter.
They become a momentary member
of the family of the departed. Troy is the city
of your childhood, now demolished utterly.

You have no photographs, and glimpse
instead reflections of its temples
in other cities, even though the windows
of their shops are full of detergent.

3

A tunnel runs underneath each street
no one knows is there and no one uses.
Every so often they cause a house
to collapse, but people soon forget.

Sometimes all the restaurants are called
the same name: *El Caballo de Troya*. But
the original, the one you went to as a child,
is always shut. Each summer at midnight

lovers circle round the block they believe
contains the restaurant where they'll meet –
they're like a dog preparing to sleep –
but they never eat. Only you can eat.

4

In the city of your childhood
you are brought breaded glands filched
from lambs' throats, you are brought
deep-fried baby cuttlefish.

In *El Caballa de Troya* you are served
two plates at once of cold custard:
this is *natillas*, perfumed with more
than cinnamon – the spice alerts you

to the fact you haven't seen the river
that no one has written about:
it fills with mist and rolls out of town.
No poet will ever see the river.

114

5

TROYTOON

Let me draw a caricature here, for caricatures
accentuate the essential.

JOSEPH BRODSKY

A Lament for Billy MacKenzie

*'...all in all, it would appear that the duende is too fragile to
survive the compulsive modernity of the music industry. In the
hysterical technocracy of modern music, sorrow is sent to the
back of the class, where it sits, pissing its pants in mortal terror.
Duende needs space to breathe. Melancholy hates haste and
floats in silence.'*

NICK CAVE

The stranger in our city's voice is dead
so keep all Dundee silent for a day,
sheathe all your spoons within their mourning cases,
fling all your florins in devalued Tay:
let every mirror hold his fourteen faces,
        our strangest voice is dead.
Our angel of the ragcart and the river,
the patron saint of tinkies, whose gold lips
could loose euphoric shrieks that split our hips –
but now he's fallen out with song forever.

He opened up the kitschy shop that lies
down crooning in our crypt-like retro hearts:
he saw the gloom in Vitriola Sundays,
the glamour of the wide-boy turning martyr,
of being but not reaching Number One –
        let lessers eat those pies.
Praise chance that once delivered that voice here,
those gorgeous tonsils, that deranging larynx:
here electronica met its finest syrinx,
but now he's broke the glass that rang so clear.

From the Hilltown to the Hilton by white car,
he sped through squalls of gull-skriek blues
and autobahned it all the way to Perth,
or spued five pernods with blackcurrant juice
projectile-style at his career's birth
        back in the Ballinard.
Cross-breeding krautrock with hick cabaret
he reared his whippet-wild songs on a diet
of lonely sardines, teaching them to shit
on dollar-deafened executives' parquet.

116

Praise to that voice, which spans the octaves as
the roadbridge spans the river's range of tides
and snell winds, bullies of Siberia.
It holds the spheres together as they gride
and squeal, that mile-wide voice, in theory our
       town's diapase, ya bass.
His gypsy holler was holy jabber-code,
our Bowie of Baldovan Terrace: hark
to Billy, Bacharach of Baxter Park.
He was the Shirley Bassey of Bonnybank Road.

He was a runaway from glassing bores,
from gnashing fathers and the ties that blind:
he married in the pyramids of Vegas
some great American bra like Hughes designed,
then took off from the girl and grew oblique as
       fear dripped from every pore.
He lost his passport, filled guitars with piss,
or caught the look he called Swiss Eye when forced
to board a plane; he endlessly divorced
his old associate: certain success.

When sales were gone, and he'd gone through the friends,
the cash and contracts like a fine tilth streams
through a riddle (money's constant, we're what flows
to deadened chore or jagged crown), news came
of Lily's cancer: when your mother goes
       childhood likes to end.
But Billy was another person from
himself – if songs are mirrors then that voice
that could sing through him seemed to eye its choices,
no longer wanting to belong to him.

Lament now for the father who must touch
a cheekbone in the barn at Auchterhouse,
who knows it in the darkness and knows why
it is so cold. Duveted in overdose,
a photo album, dumbed at thirty nine –
       lament for that numb touch.
Lament the kind of silence in that shed,
the absence of all further variation
on that one breathing theme thieved from creation:
lament MacKenzie's lovely son is dead.

Lament and flood our gritty city please:
let no more pearls form in its greedy bite
to be flung in the Tay's unhearing glass.
Dissolved, he rises like an opposite,
the Catholic in all Calvinists, the lass
        within the laddie's ease.
Lorca would know this spirit: his hair, planted
now in Balgay, sends up *duende*'s shoots.
His jawline was perfect. Let my tongue find its root in
this town's most joyous voice, its most lamented.

To Schnittke

'To the beat of the Vedic verse my mind repeated –
"Honeyed is this earth's dust."'

TAGORE

Alfred, ye sit and caa Irina thru,
still at yir desk, tears streamin doon lyk notes:
Stroke No. 3, fur Fore-brain, key of 'U'.

Thon wiz thi last o mony lasts. You wrote
tae find thi honey in symphonic dust,
while Khrennikov lashed red tape roond yir throat.

Eh nearly ken noo hoo tae be thi last
tae write in Scots, thi wey yir music kens
tae mixter-master present wi thi past.

Let aa wha crack or seek keys here tak tent
o Schnittke's wey wi whut's still crehd thi Classics –
nae language we huv learnt's left dominant

but aa's subsumed, as prose in Williams' Passaic,
or Europe glimpsed on Auden's post-war shield.
Sae passion resurrects thi glad Jurassic

and ithers' harmonies gae AWOL, yield
velociraptures and a cartoon beauty
while Scots and Volga German cross a field

haund in haund, shair that they've nae richts, jist duties.
They pass a birch that's niver kent a burd,
and waulk wi spines that don't know whit a flute is.

Eh mind thi furst bemusit time Eh heard
Life wi an Eedjit: hoo Eh couldnae hear
an opera ava, tho Vova's wurd,

this loonie Lenin's anely wurd, wiz near-
er tae meh lug than Eh kent, bein 'eh' –
aa Dundee's soond fur 'I' and 'yes' and 'er...'

Eh, well – thi alien and annealin treh
cohabitin in art, which isna aa
that different frae wirsels: relations deh

and hae tae be preserved in slaw devaul
and thocht's re-strikin – nae sic healin's done
that disnae cheenge an auld sang tae a bawl,

barbaric yawp back intae meisured tone.
Thi resurrection alters us as much
as daith: God finds oor honey in auld banes.

You worshipped in a polystylist church
His score fur aa that's human, mair that's no.
Deid stanzas and meh ain deid at your touch

belt oot thae tunes Eh didnae ken they'd know:
Young Pioneers, thir ancient fisses glow.

caa: call; kens: knows; *tak tent:* pay attention; *ava:* at all; *devaul:* a sinking or
stopping or silence, like a note's decay.

Foot of Scotland

(in memoriam the play-off for Euro 2000)

O foot of Scotland
when will ye kick thi bluidy baa?
We've waatched ye fur years noo
and ye hardly go near thi thing at aa -
so we're up against England,
loud Kevin's army,
and whit diz Paw Broon waant?
A goal-less draa.

New Hampden is seik noo
but no as seik as Billy Dodds
fur he did arise noo
and hit thi bar against aa the odds.
And so we got beat by
duff Shearer's army,
and sent them homeward
tae party oan.

Twa doon afore Wembley
then Hutchison gees England thi heid:
we've waatched ye fur years noo
and that's thi first time ye've gone in thi lead.
And so we beat them,
thi Smarmy Army,
but sent oorsels homeward
tae kick oor heels.

Aa Scotland is seik noo
and greetin in wir feechy Schemes
but we shall lie doon noo
and dream again wir sma nation's dreams
o standin against them,
cool Sven-Goran's army...
but swappin them Gallacher
fur Michael Owen.

feechy: unhygienic.

How the Word Did in Dundee

1

Wan dey in thi sixties Gode was sittin in his Ford Siesta
oan thi tap o thi Law Hill eatin his piece
when he thocht it was time fur some new wurds,
sae he rolled doon his windie
and frae thi side o his mooth slid oot, 'DUENDE'.

Large and minty white thi letters tumblet doon
thi side o thi hill stertin deevils frae thi tussocks
wi ilka dunt, and aff they went
rubbin thir inky erses tae bather thi poets.
Thi letters settlet, Hollywuid-style,
intae thi name o wur toon.

In Granadaland i thi Rovers Return
Lorca decidit tae haud his wheesht
as thi Black Banditti passed by i thi street:
it wadna dae fur thi warld tae ken
he wiz noo disguised as Stanley Ogden.

2

Thi next dey Gode wiz promenadin alang
thi Esplanade geein paiks tae thi ainguls
fishin aff thi side – ilkane tumbled i thi Tay
and mutterin arose tae shauk thir feathers dreh
i thi loabbies o thi poets.

When he gote tae thi Magdalen Green
suddenly he said 'MOJO' – and lo:
thi letters wore thi tadpole heids
of a deep rhythm o blues,
thi bandstand wiz thi soundhole o
a grecht guitar, whas neck
snaked up Blackness and stretched as faur
as Lochee whaur Mike Marra said, 'Haud oan.'

And wan fret wiz Corso Street,
anither Abbotsford Place. And therein
lived Morris Forbes wi puddin-bowl herr
and mealie-puddin fiss,
                    meh best freend frae thi skail,
and me and Keith Marshall and Michael Hammill began
at that moment tae caa him 'Mojo',
and Dundee resoundit til
oor tenement yell.

3

Oan thi third dey Gode wiz doon thi toon
lukein at thi Overgate and feelin pissed aff
wi Mary Slessor sae
he burped and oot came 'TROJAN'.
Ilka letter fused wi uts neebur intae
thi shape o a horse that cantered doon
this street that hud survehved
thi burnin o 1547 and thi massacree
by General Monk.
                    Zonked by Zeppelin
or Heinkel ut hud bideit haill,
waulked by Wedderburns and Dudley D.,
trod by Tammas Bodkin, his tabby and a labster,
sauntered by Sim thi sober, and
daundered by Dan thi Desperate,
thi route o Riddoch and thi scoot o Scrymgeour.

Oot o thi horse's mooth and uts anus forbye
craad sodger ants wi JCBs
                    and seized uts wreckin baas
and howed thi hooses doon. And thi poets commenced
thir endless waements.

And Gode luked on aa that He hud done, and said,
'EH'M THI FUCK AWA OOT O HERE!'

piece: sandwich; *dunt:* knock; *haud his wheesht:* kept quiet; *ken:* know; *paiks:*
blows; *ilkane:* each one; *mealie-puddin:* white pudding, made from oatmeal and
lard; *skail:* school; *neebur:* neighbour; *sodger:* soldier; *howed:* knocked; *waements:*
laments, elegies.

My Grandmother Is Turning into Furniture

1

There is an invisible room
I carry with me from
the ruin of her death:
I have the mirrors that
hung in that vanished flat,
the bluebell picture with,
my grandad always teased,
a squirrel that I couldn't see
hiding down its path.

I have their marriage photograph
in which her eyes have not yet seen
her husband's face in early tenderness
or later, bitten in his lungs by pain;
the face that had to tell her how
perfect her stillborn boy had been.

There is no trace of those elder eyes
that I found beautiful. Her pose
contains another beauty, so
anterior in its duck-egg cheekbones,
the elongated Russian nose,
the lips pulled almost tight with hope.

Her eyes identify it as
the icon to a happiness
that now has dissipated
into homeless air:

my grandmother is turning into furniture.

2

The two straight-spined and sag-sprung chairs
with grey- and red- and black-flecked, old
blood-toned upholstery, bare wood legs
and armrests, honey-dark worn-edged veneer:

in one she'd dover through forenoons
and in the other chat to home-helps for whom
she had already cleaned the flat
as thoroughly as she could nearly see.

They sit together in my study now
hieratic as thrones on which I read and write
as though they were a wanax's belongings
that scribes invented scripts to catalogue:

'One ebony chair with ivory back
carved with a pair of finials (?)
and with a man's figure and heifers.'

3

I never saw the baize
that would have covered it
with one definable use:
card table. So it became
everything flat that held –
a field of woodgrain oats;
a square cut from a river
full of leaves, nailed in place
on crossed dark spindly struts.
And on it were balanced cards:
the same green whale-backed pack,
the same game, *Stop the Bus*,
where now I'm float my books,
feel paper-chased by chance.

4

'One footstool inlaid with a man and a horse and an octopus
and a griffin (or a palm-tree) in ivory'
JOHN CHADWICK,
The Decipherment of Linear B

That roundish ruby velvet fading thing,
its name become hilarious to kids
and yet our filthy minds could never make
that link back then: the pouffe for her feet.

Its imitation leather top contained
a square made up of other squares, four in
each corner joined by cream rectangles and
the large red square that filled its centre,
the whole top rounded by grubby piping
as though this held alchemical meaning,
though it was just where feet went when we read
the *Sunday Post* or *Tully*, turning down
the volume on Gran and Mother arguing.

The plaited cord that held its waist was lost
in that last flit: it's left a pale ghost strip.
A cross tear in its side now shows
the water-stained pink lining and the start-
ling orange straw with which it's stuffed. And now
it squats beneath the books and mags in layers:
Longley on the cover of *Fortnight*; *Q* and *Viz*,
The Broons: The Fabulous Fifties; *The Book of Dundee*,
Dundee Prior to the Reformation; and,
indenting the leatherette, that illustrated
Iliad and *Odyssey* that I
was given when the world was still intact,
its style a hotch of pottery and mosaics:

long-fingered and red-haired Odysseus,
emerging from the ocean at Phaeacia;
Achilles, blond and savage, putting on the shield
Hephaestus made, and hunting Hector down.

5

Finally, the snap-armed tray
sprung to grip the arms of grey
armchairs that did not survive
on which my countless meals arrived,
glass beakers streaked with printed flowers:
my fingers learnt this braille of colours.

Its box showed Fifties folk who sat
and ate and watched a programme that
was one head grinning in its case,
and star and viewers shared one face.

Its plastic is that pastel blue
I now support as Lazio:
its dimpled surface has that feel
of memories smoothed until unreal
by endless repetition, like an
argument, a prayer, an icon.

She was too giving. She's become
invisible, a constant room
in which I see I must endure
her turning into furniture.

Note: wanax is the Mycenaean Greek word for 'king'.

* * *

'None of us was there to see the siege of Troy, the fall of
Constantinople, the burning of Rome, the Great Fire of London...'
BLAKE MORRISON

Troy was a small town –
we think too big now.
A few thousand looked
at massacre, not a book.

And yet its heroes
survive the sack of years,
their moods and mothers
and the moment of their deaths.

Small towns know grief's grip
and Troy did not escape:
each death was family,
the city shrank to a home.

It was lost the way we lose
our own, who are not called heroes.

The Death of Pieface

'...I inclined
To lose my faith in Ballyrush and Gortin
Till Homer's ghost came whispering to my mind
He said: I made the Iliad from such
A local row.'

PATRICK KAVANAGH

Dundee is Troy – ut's true, ask ony
   MacSchliemann o thi Tay.
Whit need huz Beanotoon o bony
   auld Archaeology?
If Achilles is real (and whit myth's phony?)
   oor cartoons can display
his modern mug, and fur meh money
   he's Dennis here, OK?
       And sae
     oor steeple staunds fur Troy.

Thi Menace hud his Myrmidons
   in jumpers striped lyk bees
launch spiky-herred assaults upon
   thi waas aroond Dundee:
amang thae sodgers Pieface shone –
   a bully, coorse an slee,
while Walter, saftest o thi sons
   o Priam, knockt his knees
      and hid,
     thi Paris of this Troy.

Lord Snooty pit oot Dennis's neb
   by actin lyk thi boss –
he wiz an aa, but sic a pleb
   as Dennis missed thi bus
tae Brains-R-Us, and fleched his ribs
   an goghlet, lukein cross –
while Desperate Dan (here Walter's sib)
   foond greenie poles tae toss
      lyk spears –
     he left aff bashin Troy.

When Dan hud driven aa thi Greeks
    back doon tae Broughty Ferry
and gey near got thir boats tae smeek
    then Pieface luked sae teary
that Dennis said, 'Ye're lassie-meek,
    yet wir dads ur slipper-merry
and faur fae deid. So whut ut's bleak
    fur Snoots? Until he's sorry
            let men
        get slauchtirt here by Troy.'

Sais Pieface, 'This is no thi punk
    aa laddies emulate –
Lord Snooty lies and greets, punchdrunk
    and aa his gang is beat;
thi Dodger couldnae jouk thae tree-trunks
    Dan flings at wir fleet,
but here's thi Menace wants tae plunk
    aff fae thi war and eat
            sliders
        upon thi beach at Troy!

'Gee me yir jumpir and thi wig
    o porpentine-sharp spikes;
Eh'll laive yir cattie – that's owre big
    fur us mere waulk-oan tykes,
but strap yir pistol tae meh leg
    and ride yir mountain bike;
and gee thae Trojans sic a fleg…'
    (He pleadit like he'd like
            tae die
        afore thi waas o Troy.)

Sais Dennis, 'Stot them frae wir ships
    and back tae Cactusville,
but listen tae yir leadir's lips
    and dinnae gang yirsel:
Apollo loves thon toon, and nips
    tae uts defence at will –
sae gee thi Gaswork Gang uts chips
    and nae mair: Gods can kill
            thae boys
        that battle here fur Troy.'

But meanwhile Biffo at thi boats
   hud dingin bells fur lugs
at aa thi stanes they threw – he gote
   his spearheid chappt aff, shrugged
an ran, sae Dennis caad his rote
   o captains – Curly, Plug
and Smiffy, dim as dildermotes –
   he powred pop inna joug
      and preyed,
      'Micht he win hame fae Troy.'

'Wha, Pieface?' pondirt Zeus. 'He'll win,
   but he's no comin hame.'
Then as a jute mill scellit men
   and weemen fae uts wame,
the Bash Street Kids and aa thir kin
   descendit oan thi team
o Trojans; Pieface geed a grin
   and wiped oot wan whas name
      wiz Smudge,
      that mingin tink o Troy.

As Smudge rejined thi flinders whaur
   he'd aye pleyed as a boy,
thi Myrmidons rejined thi war
   wi a drouth fur bluid o Troy –
jist like Last Oardirs at thi bar.
   Bluid spattirt fleesh lyk soy
in Chinese Kerry-oots, and cars
   o Trojans clogged, destroyed,
      thi trench
      en route in rout tae Troy.

(Let cynics sey Dundee's too duff,
   this locale shid be posh,
that *Novum Ilium* towers above
   such poky local trash –
let London strut, an epic toff
   wha flashes plenty dosh,
but a capital that cannae love
   uts country couldnae fash
      utsel
      tae stand in fur auld Troy.

Provincials were fooled fur lang enough
    by thon auld synecdoche
till Kavanagh caad uts gift-horse bluff –
    though horsetails cut a dash
Achilles' helmet's shoddy stuff,
    no worth meh gran's pehdish
till some wee teuchter yells, 'Here's proof!
    Eh saw him swing his cosh
        richt here.'
      Whaur Dundee diz fur Troy.

Idealists feel cartoons ur fluff,
    thi shallow-ender's splash,
draain an epic's faur mair tough
    than comics' gnash n bash –
but fechters' ethics are a laugh,
    thir consciences weel-stashed
in sketchy godes: they cut up rough,
    thir idols fix thi match.
        Heaven's
      thi deep end here in Troy.)

Noo Dan ran frae thon desperate scrum
    fur Zeus hud made him feart.
Still Pieface grinned till Little Plum
    dismoontit fae his cairt
and yelled, 'Um tribe rins lyk Red Rum
    frae whit? Um bit o skirt
that Dennis spears richt up thi bum?
    Eh'll lay'um – in um dirt!'
        And stude
      tho he wiz no fae Troy.

Noo Zeus wiz choked, fur Wee Plum wiz
    his son, thi auld femme-fooler:
Hera wad trump him and insist
    Daith stuck Plum in uts cooler.
Plum flung his tomahawk and missed,
    sae Pieface bent his ruler,
let wan ink-pellet fleh – ut kissed
    Plum's breist: nae squaw wiz crueller
        than Hera
      man-hater of aa Troy.

Plum said tae Pimple, 'Dinna let
   that bastard grab meh feather,'
then slipped his sowel frae thinkin's net.
   But bluid steeped Pimple's leathers –
he couldnae lift his bow, sae grat
   and preyed, 'Apollo, gaithir
meh strength and staunch ma cut.' Nae sweat:
   the Moose-God steghed his withers
         wi virr
     tae fecht some mair fur Troy.

He ran tae Cactusville's grecht chiefs:
   Korky, Aeneas, Dan,
said, 'Plum is deid, but dinna grieve –
   he wisnae fae your land –
jist rin and gee us nae relief,
   fur meh tribe maks a stand.'
Then Dan, in mournin, frae his nieve
   let fleh a souster and
         destroyed
     anither man at Troy.

He split thi mug o ugly Plug
   and rowed him in thi dust,
jist like a windscreen splats a bug,
   and Pieface raged and cursed,
caucht Bully Beef up by thi lug –
   guttit him wi wan thrust;
then Pimple, oan Apollo's drug
   let his lance feed uts thirst
         fur thrapples
     and dagged a few fur Troy.

But Pieface aye wiz makin groond
   wi Curly at his side –
wha geed thon Brassneck sic a wound
   he clanged oot as he died.
Aeneas cast – and missed: he mooned
   thi Trojan prince and cried,
'Ye couldnae hut a big balloon!'
   but Pieface, bluid-fou, sighed,
         'Nae wurds:
     ut's deeds that win us Troy.'

And as a river cairries noise
    sae faur-bank fowk can hear
thi haddie boxes that men hoyse
    clap doon upon thi pier,
thi stounds o battle still werr poised
    whaur Plum lay in thi steer.
But Pieface drove back Troy's maist choice
    and seized thi young brave's gear.
          Then Zeus
      seduced his thochts wi Troy.

But first he sent Apollo doon
    wi Sleep and happy Death
tae tak Plum tae his huntin groons
    and croon him wi a wreath.
Hoo mony Trojans fissed Hegh Noon
    that Pieface sent aneath?
Three times he nearly tuke thir toon
    till Apollo (oot o breath)
        said, 'NO!
      Ye wullna enter Troy.'

Sae Pieface oan thi randan pinned
    a whelk caad Billy Whizz
and laughed, 'That wiz yir second wind.'
    And Dan rubbed at his fiss.
Apollo skelped and, deaved and dinned,
    Pieface fell til his knees,
and Dan struck wance, and then he grinned.
    As life left that man's ees,
        sais Pieface,
      'First me, then you, then Troy.'

EPILOGUE
Though Troytoon's haurdly aa thi vogue
    (ut's fish-eggs tae thi lave),
Eh'm affy sorry tae thae blokes
    that kept uts kulchur safe:
apologies tae Longley, Logue,
    tae Jaynes and Robert Graves,
tae Homer tae, thon blind auld pogue,
    that DJ'd ancient raves
        and mixed
      thigither tales o Troy.

Can't Spell, Won't Spell

(On hearing of the new Scots spellchecker programme, 'Canny Scot')

Cannae spell, winnae spell – lay it oan thi line:
when it comes tae orthaegraphic skills this laddie disnae shine.
Eh cannae spell 'MaGonnagal', Eh cannae spell 'Renaissence' –
hoo Eh feel aboot this flaw is becummin raw complaysance.
If Eh cannae spell in English dae Eh huvtae spell in Scots?
Is meh joattur filled wi crosses when thi proablem is wir nots?
Wir not a singul naishun and therr's not a singul tongue:
we talk wan wey gin wir aalder and anither if wir young;
we talk diffrent in thi Borders than we dae up in thi Broch;
wir meenisters talk funny when they skate oan frozen lochs.
Huv ye seen hoo Lech Walensa's Roabin Wulliums wi a tash?
Huv ye noticed hoo Pat Lally's kinna nippy wi thi cash?
Well yi widnae if yir sittan wi yir heid stuck til a screen
Trehin tae spell oot whit ye think insteid o seyin whit ye mean.

The Death of Pieface:
129: *fleched:* scratched; *goghled:* spat; *greenie poles:* poles supporting washing lines in tenements.
130: *smeek:* smoke; *jouk:* dodge; *plunk aff:* play truant; *sliders:* ice cream wafers; cattie: catapult; *sic a fleg:* such a fright; *stot:* dash.
131: *dildermotes:* dust floating in sunlight; *scellit:* emptied out; *drouth:* thirst.
132: *teuchter:* bumpkin.
133: *grat:* wept; *virr:* vigour; *nieve:* fist; *souster:* a large rock; *rowed:* rolled; *dagged:* stabbed; *bluid-fou:* drunk with blood-lust.
134: *haddie:* haddock; *stounds:* blows; *steer:* crowd, or dust stirred up by feet; *randan:* caught up by violence or celebration; *skelped:* smacked.

Minnie the Sphinx

1

The citizens of Troytoon often visited
the basalt statue of a seated diva
wearing a Tam-o'-Shanter and striped vest
daubed red with the blood of heifers.

They petitioned her with pocket money,
and wrote their questions on the soles of slippers,
and then awaited riddles – those responses
that sometimes come to sleepers.

2

What is it that the dead remember
who are our opposites?
Everything that we forget:
who could move beneath such lumber?

How do I endure drinkupmanship
with Stetson, the two gallon hero?
Getting drunk is tender and as apt
to be abused as love.

How does Heaven decide
what age we ought to be
for the purposes of admittance
and for eternity?

Or can we be all ages
at that timeless once
or those potential selves
denied by chance decisions?

No.

Is it true that any size of octopus
can get through any size of keyhole?
That goats, with a small amount of investment capital,
will sell their own cheese by the roadside? *Yes.*

What happens when you take
the low road? *You still die.*
How was it when you first engendered night?
I encompassed nothing with my knees.

Despite the extreme unlikelihood
of me getting a shag,
tell me about the sexual position
known as 'the seated bagpipe'?

Is writing verse an oblique kind
of prophylactic?
*Does the Trojan Horse
have a wooden dick?*

3

Long after the demolishment
of that town, its refugees would wake
at night, and hear her childish croak,
its bewildered admonishment:

*Is the house there where you were born?
Is it anywhere retrievable? Are its parts
numbered, its constituents known?*

*Is there a chest filled with the clothes
that will no longer fit, that are only worn
by the scents of past decades?*

*Are your papers gathered and correct?
Your photographs dated and sorted,
their inhabitants named and forewarned?*

*Have you prepared for the questioner
who can admit you to oblivion?
Do you recognise the interrogative face*

*of one who is empowered to withhold
the rescuing waters of Lethe?*

To Robert Fergusson

*'It is recorded of the Romans that when the verdant valley
of the Tay first burst upon them, from the Hill of Moncrieff,
they cried out, 'Lo another Tiber! See a second Martian plain!'*
ALEXANDER B. GROSART

Thi daftest o deys atween a heap
o festivals is when Eh keep
meh wurd tae skell ye frae yir sleep
     and yell in yir skull,
'Here comes yir tribute frae a creep –
     ut's lang and dull!'

Atween meh duck-bunged Yule and that
dank Hogmillennium o tat,
thi shampers and firewarks equally flat:
     oor kulchur's treh
at haein fun – lyk spaein thi cat
     or a turd in a peh.

Atween thi nicht that Scots forgot
(St Andrew's) and thir loss o plot
that mairks thi birth o Mister Sot
     (that's Rab, yir namesake),
Eh blaa oot lines lyk a neb blaas snot
     jist fur yir fame's sake.

Atween a thoosan years o gore,
and, wi a glisk at Grozny, a thoosan more,
atween a parliament o whores
     and independence,
Eh scrunt and chap at yir coffin's door
     lyk a mim defendant.

Insteid o aa thae legal drones
fur you tae copy, here's a poem
that micht elicit ghaistly groans
     and gar ye shift
yir young man's under-usit bones:
     meh gab's your gift.

But lyk thi gant atween thae times –
thi fairs, thi races – in your rhymes,
and oor homogeny o mimes
          and thon Dumbo dome,
ye'll find meh crambo bad as crimes
          against garden gnomes.

Compared tae Garioch's canny habbie
meh stanzas drehv lyk a weel-tipped cabbie:
whaur Boab turns terse is whaur Eh'm blabby –
          Ach, Eh'm aa effect –
whit Eh mak tolter he kept slabby,
          he showed respect.

But Eh shair nae britherhood wi you
at laist o thi kind Boab Garioch knew
o vennel, brae and brat-time view
          o thi Seat and Forth –
tho Dundee High and St Andrews drew
          you further north.

Yet that's lyk Wallace: wha can find
a whiff o hum doon Dundee's wynds,
thi saviour o aa Scottishkind
          wha geed Selby paiks?
Noo aa that Wallace brings tae mind's
          thi Land o Cakes

– and Gibson gibbering like an ape
oan Freedom and pair Scoatlan's rape
while Pat McGooghan peels a grape
          and skites a midge,
Mel's prick is proven Oscar-shaped
          at Stirlin Bridge.

Tho there's yir learnin at thi Uni,
thae years that left yir leths sae puny
and mebbe helped yir harns turn loony
          at thi thocht o Hell,
thi leir that sticks lyk hair wi chewnie –
          Eh ken that well.

Not whit a college crehs success
nor recognised noo by oor Press
as Scots – atween them nanethiless
        nor heich nor hard,
Horace and Leith shares your address,
        oor double bard.

And that's whaur Eh wauk up: tae feel
thi caller splash o verse congeal
thi current notion naethin's real
        but prose schemes whaur
McDivots rant and writhe lyk eels
        in grit and glaur.

You brocht tae *Luckie Middlemist*'s,
whaur poetry lay panned and pished,
lyk pandour eysters, lines sae kissed
        wi that dose o saut
crehd 'history' – we cam alist,
        stood up, and wrote

fur Mnemosyne, that usefu muse,
wha minds us tae pit oan wir trews
afore we laive thi publishin hoose:
        there have been books
in which oor ancients sang thi blues
        while we squeezed plooks.

Although wir journos cannae read
and Jockstar belters lost in greed
think punters shid furget thi leid
        o Henryson,
Dunbar and Douglas haud a gleid
        that burns thi tongue.

Oor nation's literature extends
thru dialects and dowie pends
tae depths whaur divots get thi bends
        while readin Hogg,
and heichts whaur Hugh MacDiarmid tends
        tae pop thir lugs.

Sae Fergusson, oor double bard,
you kent tae pley thi joker's card
when Reekie's ghaists – they micht hae jarred –
    talked politics;
and hung auld Hector's tag oan a scarred
    drunk bein sick.

Frae Musselbrugh tae Tuscany,
frae Tiber til thi Tay, ye'd pree
thi prospect syne tak aff thi gree –
    nor gowdspink nor
thi catwalk-flichty butterflee
    wad you ignore.

And keepied up thi wurds sae well
fae Robin Gibb tae pair Jock Bell,
wha passed tae Sawney, fa aa could tell
    wiz Aiberdeenie:
he sliced leid at thi auld Tron Bell
    lyk Paolo Maldini.

Frae Buchan boadies, browster wives,
frae tinkler billies, shairpenin knives,
frae tonguey weemen, drinkin dives
    tae Marion on
thi cuttie stool – you plucked oor lives
    frae Acheron.

Ye mairried Pluto's dreary toun
tae Reekie in hur broukit goun
o wurds lyk snortirs hingin doon
    or Watson's shrood
fur ainly wurds when ye're in thi groond
    are ony good.

There's thirty-odd that Burns hiz borraed
that you and Allan Ramsay quarried
frae lodes and seams fur whilk auld Murray'd
    near OEDed:
a hundred, Pound said, 's aa thi hurried
    warld poet'll need.

You kept thi door stapped open atween
thi antique and thi eident scene
of Embro's prime, sae baith can glean
      frae thi ither's hairst,
sae we can free whit still can mean
      noo thi doorframe's burst.

And sae thi strain o stentin past
thi een o ithers telt at last:
thi gardyloo o hellfire waasht
      yir mind til thru it
drows and jowes, wanwordy, thrasht
      a clamihewit.

Lyk Burns' bairns' births, maist daith's unplanned:
yours fell atween oblivion and
oor grubbin need tae understand,
      and wha's tae say
hoo late sall lowe thi dim's demand –
      biography?

Young Fergusson under a drumly mune's
heard John Broon o Haddington denoonce
aa ribaldry and's felt thi poonce
      o thi Bible's wecht:
uts black knock is thi worst o stounds
      whaur his wits are steghed.

Young Fergusson wan nicht is fleggit
by a ghaist baith fell and fower-leggit
wha claas a speug and trehs tae dreg ut
      oot frae uts cage
thi burd's skreiks tear his wits near nekkit
      wi haly rage.

Young Fergusson faas doon thi sterrs
and cracks his harns ayont repairs,
and Darien hears his final prayers
      devoid o suss –
and Hugh MacD, tae muss his hairs,
      fell aff a bus.

Thi Clapham omnibus, nae doot:
he landit oan his lyric snoot
and banged, fowk sey, his rhythms oot –
          they dwyned tae prose
as gyte as you or goons that toot
          shite up thir nose.

But Eh wad airgue Mister Grieve
could wipe mair verse aff oan his sleeve
than them wha waant us tae believe
          that he turned sad
not in thir nelly puff could scrieve –
          ut's them that's mad.

And sae wi you, yir granes and greets,
ye nearies til a Northern Keats,
ye poet o the clartit streets
          and ragman's cart,
oor Jimmy Dean o thi canty beats
          oor ain Kit Smart.

Lyk Cowper, Clare or Thomas Gray
yir sanity wiz wede away
by trehin tae turn whit people say
          tae somethin rare,
hud you recovered, we wad hae
          a rivin quair.

But jist as paper's prone tae burn
we literary Scots are prone tae yearn,
wha tint thi pleys o Wedderburn
          and thi myths o thi Picts:
you drank Leith's waaters at yir turn
          and crossed thi Styx.

Yet fur twa years ye swyved thi city
ejaculatin verse sae glitty
ut faithered mony an urban ditty
          lyk this wan noo;
ye dodged thi blackest o banditti –
          ahent yir broo.

Ye geed us aa a double gift:
a language able aye tae shift
frae causey stane tae streamery lift,
        sae, Fergusson,
Eh hail ye in that speerit drift –
    and sae ye're gone.

To Robert Fergusson:

138: *skell:* spill, rouse; *neb:* nose; *glisk:* glimpse; *scrunt:* scratch; *chap:* knock; *mim:* restrained, affected; *gar:* make.

139: *gant:* yawn, gap; *crambo:* rhymes, doggerel; *tolter:* unbalanced; *vennel:* narrow lane; *brae:* hill; *paiks:* blows (William Wallace stabbed Selby, the son of the English captain of Dundee Castle, to death in a street brawl around 1290); *skites:* smacks; *leths:* limbs; *harns:* brains; *chewnie:* chewing gum.

140: *caller:* fresh, invigorating; *glaur:* mud; *pandour eysters:* large succulent oysters caught near Prestonpans at the doors of the salt pans; *saut:* salt; *cam alist:* were revived; *trews:* trousers; *leid:* language; *gleid:* glowing coal; *dowie pends:* dismal alleys.

141: *pree:* taste, test; *syne:* then; *tak aff the gree:* extract the best; *browster wives:* women who brewed and sold ale; *cutty stool:* the place in a church where those guilty of misconduct were obliged to sit; *broukit:* dirty, streaked; *snortirs:* beads of snot dangling from the nose.

142: *stapped:* forced; *eident:* bright, living; *hairst:* harvest; *stenting:* stretching, straining; *een:* eyes; *gardyloo:* warning that waste water etc was about to be poured into the street from an upper storey (from *gardez l'eau*), here transferred to the substance itself; *drows:* spasms of anxiety; *jowes:* judders; *wanwordy:* unworthy, inappropriate; *clamihewit:* drubbing or hubbub; *lowe:* flame; *drumly:* gloomy, troubled; *stounds:* blows; *steghed:* stuffed; *fleggit:* scared; *speug:* sparrow; *skreiks:* screams; *haly:* holy.

143: *dwyned:* shrivelled up, fell away; *gyte:* mad; *in their nelly puff:* in their life-time; *granes:* groans; *greets:* crying fits; *clartit:* muddied; *canty:* lively; *wede away:* withered; *rivin:* full or bursting; *quair:* book; *tint:* lost; *swyved:* copulated with; *glitty:* fertile; *ahent:* behind; *broo:* brow.

144: *causey stane:* cobblestone; *streamery lift:* sky filled with the Aurora Borealis; *speerit:* spirit.

At MacDiarmid's Tomb:

with acknowledgements to *The Geology of The Neighbourhood of Langholm*, by G.I. Lumsden, W. Tulloch, M.F. Howells, and A. Davies; *Orkney & Shetland*, by W. Mykura; and *Geology and Scenery in Scotland*, by J.B. Whittow.

At MacDiarmid's Tomb

The base is layered Scottish Ordovician and Silurian
greywackes from the Langholm area, siltstones, mudstones,
and thin bands of shale of Wenlock age, carrying graptolites.
The greywackes have weathered to a greenish-grey;
they are coarse, with a variegated appearance due to
the presence of red, brown and black chert.
Quartz is the predominant mineral, generally angular
to subangular, its peripheries often full
of small micaceous intrusions. Undulose
strain extinction and granulation are common.

Feldspar is always subordinate to quartz in a true greywacke.
The fragments are smaller, less angular, with a turbid relief.
Plagioclase of albite-oligocase composition
and potash feldspar are present;
granophyric and myrmekitic inclusions
and perthitic intergrowths also appear.
Muscovite plates are invariably present, showing
strained optical characters; small sericite flakes are
an important part of the matrix.

The sides consist of Whalsay's highly metamorphosed
homogeneous pelitic and semipelitic gneisses
with much quartzite and some impure limestone.
Nearly all this has been intensely migmatised
and is now coarsely crystalline. There is abundant
garnet and kyanite, cut by numerous
small granite intrusions.

The lid is basic pyroxene-andesites and olivine-basalts
with a laccolite intrusion of felsite.
The sedimentary layers under this include
a thick basal greywacke conglomerate, which also contains
clasts of pebbly grit, chert, jasper and acid igneous rock.
Greywacke sequences are generally lacking in shelly fossils
but these mudstones and conglomerates from around Biggar
contain over 20 species of brachiopods and 12 of trilobites.
The lavas are overlain by a final layer
of ashy and flaggy Old Red Sandstone.

The Great Camperdown Breakout

*'A Dundee City Council spokesman described the wallabies
as not dangerous animals.'*

THE COURIER, 15.7.99

Tho Camperdoon Park's a rare auld zoo
nae baist, Eh think, gets pissed in there:
haal up a chair and Eh'll tell ye hoo
thir wallabies went oan thi tear.

Fehv broon, twa grey, and yin aa white
these drongoes wi a drouth fur yill
louped owre thi fence at thi fit o thi night –
thir splores and spills ur aa meh tale.

They scellit, lyk *The Great Escape,*
tae spite thae parkies in pursuit:
wore shellsuits tae disguise thir shape
but luked a wee bit, well, hirsute.

No that ye'll no find men that hairy
if you sup beer in fair Lochee,
in Kirkton, tae, or in St Mary's
fowk let thir follicles flow free.

But when fehv big broon wallaby bucks
hopped intae a bar in mirror specs,
there werr as mony muttirt 'fuck!'s
as oardirs fur pints o Fower X.

This wiz thi *Sportin Lodge,* whaur lads
ur not averse tae fisticuffs –
as bairns they'd battled in thir tansads,
but marsupials haund oot muckle duffs.

on the tear: off for an extended session of drinking and misbehaving; *splores:*
adventures; *scellit:* scattered; *parkies:* park attendants; *tansads:* prams; *muckle:*
strong.

Wee manky Mike wiz furst tae swing,
and duntit thi snot fae a broonie's neb.
Ut geed a 'Tut', syne sic a ding
Mike's een werr frehd lyk drappit eggs.

Thi boys piled in, thi wallabies
jist helt thir pints abune thir heids,
and wi thir tails they walloped these
sons o Lochee wi nae remeid.

They lunted owre the killiemahou,
got lowndered by lubbards, but paikit thi punks,
till mamikeekies, bluid and spew,
droukit this drave o roos and drunks.

Meanwhile a mannie, waur fur wear,
wiz stottin hame fae thi *Golden Pheasant*
when he saw a grey thing that lukeit mair
alien than usual in Harestane Crescent.

(Some sey these pubs ur nae langer there
and new wans hae sprung up i thi meantime,
while ithers feel thi haill affair
tuke place in an alcoholic Dreamtime.)

Ut spangit alang thi lane sae fast
ut seemed a ghaistly meteorite:
he stauchirt in thi hoose aghast
till his wife explained he wiz talkin shite.

Amanda awoke in Claverhoose Court
tae see a Greychops appear tae stare
thru'ur windie, then drap – wance mair fur sport,
then aff – but she wiz oan thi fourth flair.

A baker's drehvur in Edison Place
hud seen a grey, lyk young Amanda:
he'd backed tae thi circle and therr werr thi police –
sae he telt a Panda he'd spottit a kanga.

neb: nose; *een:* eyes; *drappit eggs:* eggs dropped into a pan; *remeid:* remedy, relief;
lunted: sprang; *killiemahou:* uproar; *lowndered:* beaten severely; *lubbards:* louts;
paikit: struck; *mamikeekies:* smart blows; *droukit:* drenched; *stottin:* staggering
uncontrollably from side to side of the road; *spangit:* sprang; *stauchirt:* staggered.

Thi parkies hud coarnered in Clatto Wuid
thae reprobates that bust up thi bar
when Doonfield Golf Course caaed that they hud
thir grey mate gaun roond at fehv under par.

Nae clubs as ye've guessed, he jist yaised his tail,
and blootert thi baas at thi boys in blue
till Tayside's finest turnit pale,
hid ahent shields and let him pley through.

Thi parkies flung nets aa nicht, and missed
till thi wallabies werr sae whammilt wi spreeins
(and mair by noo nor normal pished)
they gote caucht by these fishers of antipodeans.

Aa but thon brankless blank ane that
meh smarter hearers may still mind o
thi whitely wan, thon anti-bat,
oor flit-by-nicht Dick Whitterton – kind o –

Ned Kelter o thi Seedlie Hills,
thi wallaby that won awa,
that wool Houdini-whale whas skills
huv made wee Ahabs of us aa.

Snow Joey, hoo yir freends noo languish
and gee wir visitors thi Skippy finger:
they say 'Come hame,' in sober language –
thir heids ur nippin fae thon humdinger.

Thon reilibogie really blew
their brains and oors oot Alice Springs-way:
thir pooches ur fuhl o Irn Bru,
thir mooths o tarmac fae thi Kingsway.

But still Eh see him in a dwaum
gae hoppin owre thi purple braes,
thon aboriginal wee bam:
Eh hope he stubs his fuckin taes.

---

blootert: hit very hard; *ahent:* behind; *whammilt:* overwhelmed; *spreeins:* drunken riotous behaviour; *brankless:* unrestrained; *reilibogie:* tumult, disorder; *dwaum:* dream; *bam:* nutter, git.

Through the Keyhole

Kate, oor haimald shrew, oor Kennedy,
in keyholed miniskirt and legendary leggins,
        oor probe, oor 'Oh?' oor sis,
oor Mata Hari in X-ray specs,
oor sharpest neb, oor gar-ma-true,
oor mislippened wan, oor 'Hist!'
oor nine-tale-teller and traducer,
oor birler o thi stories, oor rumour-abuser,
oor kuriosity, oor resurrectit kat, oor krazy eye,
oor sin, oor noise, oor surety.

Thi keyhole is yir lanely hieroglyph:
an armless ankh, a shaven heid, black skirt,
nae ankles showing; thi blankety-blank,
thi pupil wi a leak, lightbulb dispensin gloom,
duck foot o soot, a distillation of bedroom;
        thi original question
oor fantasies ur pressed within.
Whit wiz it that ra butler saw in you?

Your nose is thi gristle key, your eye
        thi tumbler o wir secrets' locks,
your lug deciphers ony hertbeats hidden by
oor shirty skirtin boards, oor plaistery wark,
oor skewin o thi picture's rails,
oor heidboard's morse or thi vaginal bells
        in which thi toilin clapper tolls.
Thi genetic codes of aa slugs and snails
are oan thi tip of your tattlin tongue
alang wi wir sugary spice-rich wrangs:
giraffish ut will swally aa
thi acacia thorns of auld scold's masks
        and touch us whaur we're quick.

        Kassandra of oor psychic sump,
oor lady of thi well, thi base camp of oor relief,
        hoo can you iver be believed?

NOTE: 'Kate Kennedy' is a bell in St Leonard's College, St Andrews.

149

The Red Cludgie
(for Stuart MacHardy)

Thi hert's a cludgie, flush and blub:
MacHardy in a Glescae pub
recordin fur a radio show
thi kind o Scots we ainly know
because we're baith frae wur West End.
Time tae rehearse whut we've aye kent:
Haakhill, Tait's Lane and Corso Street,
then Peddie, Annfield, Blackness – beat
the drum o names' belangin, think
o sandstane's wame and hae a drink.
Hoo mony shillins wad ye pey
tae mak time turn thi ither wey?
In increments of echty, fehv
(or six) and deid shoaps come alehv,
auld wifies scrub deid closies' stairs
tae life, like rubbers in reverse
they fret thi steps lyk empty jotters
fur errors by thir sons and dochters.
Thir waashin hings fae chapped-doon masts:
thir greenie poles sail hame wir pasts.
Like waatchin whaleboats rax thir jetties
we see bairns pley oan sunken pletties.

And noo a whirlpool sterts tae birl
and swallies up wir ancient warld
we'd virtually rebuilt fae beer,
and couthy crack sterts turnin weird:
whaur did your grannie bide in aa this
suburb o slibberkin Atlantis?
In Corso Street? Well, mine did tae.
Whit number? Fourteen? Whit dje say?
Aaricht, let's sort this oot: whit land?

cludgie: toilet; *echty shillin:* beer; *closie:* entrance and stairs of a tenement; *greenie poles:* poles with several pulleys attached for hanging out laundry; *rax:* reach; *pletties:* balconies; slibberkin: sleek, glossy, a term of endearment, also slippery, mutable.

Thi tap an aa? Noo understand
we kent that we werr proximate
but noo we're actin kinna blate:
yir roots ur things that shidnae shift
but here time's geed a shooglin gift.
Whit flat wiz yours, thi left or richt?
(aaready kennin – still thi fricht
o findin oot withoot nae closure
oor faimlys' doubled-up exposure.)
Domestic duties, acts of love
are overwritten, pushed tae shove:
thi weelkent fisses scribblet oan
by profiles we huv niver known.

Because ye're sober you'll huv got
thi answer tae oor loss o plot –
dope-dozent in oor youth wir wits
werr freakin oot lyk weans wi nits –
but we're no eildins: Stuart huz
a few mair stoaps upon his bus.
His fowk hud flittit, mine moved in:
sic occupations ur nae sin.
Well hae a dram, boys, don a cardie,
we've solved thi mystery o thi MacHardies –
until Eh tuke this story hame
and Gran revealed thir secret shame.
Fur they werr Catholic Communists
jist like meh faither – aften pished
and plottin fur thi overthrow
o prods. And did she ken them? No,
but when Granda muved in wir budgie
he foond they'd left a penntit cludgie.
Whit disrespectfu colour? Reid
as rags, as flags, as people bleed.
Still, eftir coontless coats, ut blushed
whaur, innocent fur years, Eh'd flushed.

---

land: a floor of a tenement; *blate:* reluctant; *shooglin:* nudging, destabilising; *dozent:*
stupefied; *eildins:* of the same age; *flittit:* moved house.

Sciffy

Ilka stane huz steyed in place
ye've sciffied in thi Tay
or else thi tide hiz rowled thum roond
a few fit either wey.

Sae aa thi bairns and lads and men
that threw in ilka stane
ur still stuck til thir throwein arc
tho aa ye've been is gane.

Or else thi graff and grind o years
huz polished thum tae air
thru whilk thi gulls and craws aa pass
and niver seem tae tear.

And aa these years thi glitter sits
oan ilka wave and niver fits.

sciffy: to skim flat stones across the surface of a stretch of water, also, to point to
where something is hidden, by stroking one palm across the other.

Elegy for My Grandmother

You seemed to leave us by degrees
deliberately, to inure
us to your last departure.

First you were decanted from
that top floor flat, my other home
(post-war, a touch up from tenements).

Then you elected to flit
from its ground floor substitute, still in
the constancy of Corso Street,

the name of which – Italian
doppeling English like its pairs of flats –
was like the mirrors on your wall,

deco-edged, wedding gifts reflecting
back the Thirties. You moved to
that hermit's room in Harefield House,

as though deserving nowhere bigger
in which to die. We emptied out
your home while you began to lose

your keys, your stockings, or your change:
anything your mind could suppose
was being stolen when it was,

I thought, you narrowing your range
to leave possessions out. I got
you shifted to a decent room:

you sent your creased hand bruising down
the sides of such familiar armchairs for
things that were never missing,

just the memory being squashed
out, just your sharpness, your account
of pennies nudging out of shape

as the meningioma grew,
a clumsy thumb bashed by
a cartoon hammer, bulging bigger,

blotting out more, until your balance
went, and one eye began to skew
from what was before you, Ben Turpin-like.

And then the skull I'd watched advance
through millimetres of its thinning flesh
for twenty years was clear to all.

You went to wards you never knew
you wouldn't leave, where you were told
your setting every quarter hour,

so near to Balgay Cemetery, where
your brother lies. And when I left
for air, walking past the warehouse-

cum-chapel where the bodies go,
I couldn't find his grave. You slid
from ward to terminal ward as

the act of breathing was reduced
to gasps and ratchets, clutchings and
embraces for our best attempts

at language who had never touched
to show our love. You asked, but how
could I take you away to where?

Easier to kiss and let you go
and hope you wouldn't be there when
I came the next time. *The Poseidon*

Adventure blared unwatched upon
the TV in your ward; I went
for a walk with my father to

escape from the flood of upturned yells,
and didn't say goodbye, and left.

* * *

'*D'oh!*'

'*My own intent now is to tell you of Troy*
of the stour and the strife when that town was destroyed.
Years have flown past since that fight and that fall:
it moved men then, now it's moved out of mind,
though many thought wise thought it worthy of words
and left it in Latin that few of us learn.

Then prize-winning poets polished their speech
with fables and falsehood and fumbled the tale,
made more of some matters than masters would
or looked at too little, lost sight of the whole.
Among this muddle one man comes to mind
called Homer – held to be wholesome, a doer,
the dearest of all while his days endured –
from Greece, and so a great friend of the Greeks.
Never before sailed such fleets of fibs.
He turned off the truth and is not worth your trust.
I've no time to tell of his travesties here,
how gods fought in fields, as though they were folk –
elementary errors that everyone knows
since poets I prize have proven him wrong,
Ovid and others, that always were honest,
virtuous Virgil, his every note noble –
these damn and deny this dull man's drafts.'

(from *Gest Hystoriale of the Destruction of Troy*)

The Fall of the House of Broon

*'Quhat cite can indure quhen it is siegit and assailyeit
without be enemies; and within the cite ringis mortal weyr
amang the governours and inhabitantis?'*

WEDDERBURN, The Complaynt of Scotlande

*'Unslothful Aeneas, brother of hovering Cupid,
carrying your Trojan relics on banished ships...'*

TIBULLUS, translated by Philip Dunlop

Oor Wullie sat in Carthage Toon – a kind of place,
like Glasgow – gazing on the harbouring fair face
of Dido, Helen-envious, who showed no interest
in his now midnight-busting tale of how the best
of cities once got burnt, or whether such a town
had ever quite existed, half-tune, half-cartoon.
He had to skip where Walter skewered Dennis with
a dahlia for an arrow – any famous death
just made her yawn, as did the yarn of Roger's dodge:
the fabricated horse where English troops could lodge,
the fleet's retreat round Budden and the brilliant lie
Sir Andrew Dudley told to get the Horse inside.
It was, he claimed, cram-packed with Bibles and such tracts
as would ensure a Reformation built on facts,
persuading radicals like Robert Wedderburn
to take assurance of protection, if Lord Arran
sent Catholic French to Troy's relief, since Mary had
already fled to France, however roughly wooed...
– At this Queen Dido jerked awake and asked the boy,
'Were we not talking here of Helen, and of Troy?
And, since we're at it, why would cartoons hurt their home?
And when' (politely) 'might Oor Wullie leave for Rome?'
But Thistlehead had not yet told of Laocoön
that old priest Dundee's faithful knew as Granpaw Broon:
he'd stuck a spear into the Horse's hardboard side
and said, 'Nae psalters Eh ken clatter as ye read.'
So Robert claimed these wore the Armour of the Word
but then the Broons' young twins hacked at it with their swords.
'Is this,' asked Dido, 'where big snakes rear from the sea
and fatally flamenco with our Doubtful Three?'

'If ships are serpents,' Wullie said, 'we're in concordance:
the Mary Hambroughe blew those boys to bits with ordnance,
and then the Ager barked shot out and hit the priest.'
'And then the town was burnt and gave your tongue a rest.'
'Tyndale and Frith's translation, and a larger fleet,
they promised, neared the firth – a lie wrapped in a threat.
The town surrendered and was ruled from Broughty Castle:
its folk returned the shot to save the English hassle.
And for a year Dundee gave English ships a berth,
and Lord Argyle's relief was bribed to go to Perth.
And Dudley told his noble boss the River Tay
was filled with fish and ships and Scotsmen who'd betray
their city for ideas *or* for gold – and here
Queen Dido yelled, 'Just hit the sack some time this year!'
But now Oor Wullie whispered with reluctance, forced
to tell what broke his voice and bleached his thistle hairs:
'I saw that desperate man who died in Troy's defence
brow clubbed and ankles pierced, that huge heart lanced,
wrapped in his dust-clogged shroud, and in my stupid sleep
forgot he was a rubbed-out sketch: how could he weep
and warn me that the clarity of final sights
would wake me soon? Unless we scribbles shade the light
enabling you to see those inner turbines grind
out griefs and lust – you are machined to simple ends –
why should two drawings mourn to know excision came?'
(That Dido shed a tear at this made her ashamed.)
'One night in which a city loses to the pyre
all relics and all records echoes other fires.
The French relief advancing, English cannon lathered
the town with that same shot its citizens had gathered,
and burnt it as they fell back to the Ferry's fort:
in this same instant Greeks sneaked through the Scaean Port
and murdered Trojans' first security of dreams,
and so the Janissaries overran Byzantium
a hundred years before Dundee's first fall, and so
a century fled in that single furnace glow
that scorched out Wedderburn's ideals and home and sent
out to a cindered nation his devout *Complaynt*,
and we ran to defend St Mary's Tower from
Cromwell's gross general, Monk, mind set on righteous pogrom
just as his troopers were on looting's quick-fit profit,
for greed and zeal both share this trait: they know no surfeit.'

'And which delightful cartoon creature have you saved
to send these several peoples to their common grave?'
'Imagine, Queen, a river filled with dog-bowls, turds,
fragments of kennel, thigh-bones, all half-chewed, half-charred
by this serrated bubble, this blank silhouette:
behold the dog that's a cartoonist's ragged shout,
Lewis's Tyronic grin, a guillotine of tooth,
the snapping jaws of porcelain, that trap, the proof.'
'What?' Dido rubbed her kohl and, ordering coffee, moaned,
'That poodle-thing?' 'An Abyssinian tripe-hound,'
Wullie corrected. 'Neoptolemus of towsers,
Pyrrhus of pooches, first to bite a Trojan's trousers
and then the leg, clean through, in vengeance for his master.
He set the damp straw in the tower and smoked its rafters.
When Keyhole Kate ran out he choked her in the chapel,
and when the governor cried quarter, bit his thrapple.
Gnasher commanded all of quhatsomever sex
put to the sword or shot, then Fido went for Rex.'
'How many women?' Dido asked. 'Two hundred died
and children: bones surround the tower while inside
the walls are cratered with the executions' plooks
and Monk's men took twa hundred thousand pounds of loot.'
'I've heard appalling lists like these drawn up of cities
without the use of myth to gloss atrocities.'
'Drogheda, Nanking, Grozny, South Manhattan, Troy:
what's done by wholly humans to humanity
enacts with blunt reductiveness that butcher's myth
that lesser things need neither legends nor to live.
But if contempt degrades our myths into cartoons
let high and low art's fall be seen here in the Broons.'
'So, Priam and his sons? And, is it, Hecuba?'
'What's she to you? She was Maw Broon to us, and Paw
the faither of our tribe. To Glebe Street Gnasher ran,
a sanctuary to Trojans since our town began;
to us the street of streets, where Aggie lived with Dan,
where Hecuba now chitters, clutching at her clan
as Horace flees, his books poor armour, and, struck down,
lies writhing at his father's feet, the last of sons
that dynasty dreamed futures for, for Joe and Hen
were killed before, as were (unknown to Maw) her twins.
Now Daphne and the half-grown bairn would be the hures
of the Achaean lords, and kneel to scrub their stairs.'

'What happened to the normal-looking one, the beauty?'
'Maggie? Did she exist? A goddess of our city.'
'Now half-forgotten in this massacre of icons.'
'Which I could not prevent. My friends all fell, each seeking
their own death with their town's. Wee Eck, Fat Boab, all met
the end that kept a sword's length off from my harsh fate.
For Dan's ghost told me I must witness everyone be killed
and only in the telling witness Troy rebuilt.
And so it was I found myself in that dark close,
the stairwell strewn with ash and glass and sodden clothes,
the weeping from above the only living note,
ascending with the smoke and bile mixed in my throat.
The broken door, the lobby bloodied and, estranged
from everything but pity, huddled by the range
the headless trunk of Priam on his young son's corpse.'
'What did you do?' 'There was a nothing that elapsed
somehow, and then a thought: I still could have a father,
a child, my wife. I ran to see what I could gather.'
'What did you find?' 'Some part of them, and that my flight
diffused a human space to what you've heard tonight:
caricatures of loved souls, doodles of a home.'
Dido repeated gently, 'Wullie, leave for Rome.'

ACKNOWLEDGEMENTS

Acknowledgements are due to the editors of the following pub-
lications in which some of these poems first appeared: *Acumen, The
Devil, Fulcrum, The Guardian, Impresiones, The Keralan Journal of
Literature & Aesthetics, Love for Love* (Polygon, 2000), *The Paper,
Poetry Review, Pitch, The Red Wheelbarrow, riverrun, Stand* and
Staying Alive: real poems for unreal times (Bloodaxe Books, 2002).

Some poems from 'The Praise Book of East Shields' have appeared
on the CD-ROM *Book of the North*, have been set to music by Keith
Morris, performed in Live Theatre, Newcastle and in Sunderland,
and webcast as part of *Livestock from Ark*, Stockton-on-Tees.

'To Robert Fergusson' was commissioned by the St Andrews
festival, StAnza, broadcast on BBC Radio 3, and appears in *Robert
Fergusson*, edited by Robert Crawford (Tuckwell Press, 2002)

I would like to thank the British Council for the trips to Moscow,
St Petersburg, Alacala de Henares and Valladolid which inspired
some of the poems in this book. My particular thanks go to Sasha
Dugdale, Elizabeth White, Ricardo Sola and Pilar Abad García. I
am also grateful to my former colleagues in the Department of
Creative Writing at Lancaster University for their support, in
particular Linda Anderson; and to Claire Malcolm and the staff at
New Writing North for their patient work on *Book of the North*.

www.ingramcontent.com/pod-product-compliance
Lightning Source LLC
Jackson TN
JSHW020020141224
75386JS00025B/627

* 9 7 8 1 8 5 2 2 4 6 0 3 7 *